CXC EXCEL SERIES

PRACTICE PAPERS FOR CXC SPANISH

Paulette Ramsay
Anne María Bankay

REVISED SYLLABUS

LMH Publishing

© 1998, Dr. Paulette Ramsay
© 1998, Dr. Ann Maria Bankay

First Edition, 1998
10 9 8 7 6 5 4 3 2
Revised Edition 1999
10 9 8 7 6 5 4 3 2 1
Reprint 2000
10 9 8 7 6 5 4 3 2
Reprint 2001
10 9 8 7 6 5 4 3 2 1

All rights reserved. No part of this book may be reproduced, stored in a retrieval system, or transmitted, in any form or by any means, electronic, mechanical, photocopying, recording, or otherwise, without the prior written permission of the publisher(s) or author(s).

The publishers have made every effort to trace the copyright holders but if they have inadvertently overlooked any, they will be pleased to make the necessary arrangements at the first opportunity.

If you have bought this book without a cover you should be aware that it is "stolen" property. The publisher(s) / author(s) have not received any payment for the "stripped" book, if it is printed without their authorization.

Illustrations and images: Reproduced with permission from Microsoft Corporation.

Cover Design: Julia-Mei Tan

Typesetting by: Wayne Ho Sang Printing Services Ltd., Kingston 5.

Published by: LMH Publishing Limited
7 Norman Road,
LOJ Industrial Complex
Building 10
Kingston C.S.O., Jamaica
Tel: 876-938-0005; 938-0712
Fax: 876-928-8038
Email: lmhpublishing@cwjamaica.com

Printed and bound by Lightning Source Inc., USA

ISBN 976-610-178-7

FOREWORD

"Por fin" a text in answer to such concerns as, 'What is this new CXC syllabus?', and 'How does one prepare for the examination?' This book is certainly the reliable companion of teachers and students who will face the challenges of the CXC Examination with confidence and ultimately with success. The practice papers are extensive and well thought out with a variety of themes that should capture any student's interest. This text will undoubtedly be well received by teachers of Spanish. ¡Adelante!

Ouida Lodge-Jones
President – Spanish Teachers' Association
Jamaica

ACKNOWLEDGEMENTS

The authors would like to thank Miss Mariana González and Mrs. Aracelis Anedu for their help with proof-reading. Special thanks to Miss Althea Aikens for typing. Thanks also to José Francisco Avila of Garífuna World Inc. for permission to use information on the Garífuna culture.

CONTENTS

	Page
Listening Comprehension Basic and General	1
Situations Basic and General Proficiency	43
Letters / Dialogues / Compositions General Proficiency	55
Reading Comprehension Basic Proficiency	65
Reading Comprehension General Proficiency	95
Directed Writing General Proficiency	113

LISTENING COMPREHENSION

BASIC AND GENERAL PROFICIENCY

COMMON SECTION

Candidates are required to select responses (multiple choice) to questions based on a continuous passage read in Spanish.

Questions and multiple choice answers are in English.
This section corresponds to **Paper 1 Section 4 and is worth 20 marks.**

MIGUEL GOES TO CAMP

BASIC QUESTIONS

Part A

1. What was Miguel looking forward to next weekend?

    A. His first camp.
    B. Buying his new knapsack.
    C. Buying his new sleeping bag.
    D. His first free weekend.

2. What did his mother purchase for him?

    A. A knapsack.
    B. A sleeping bag.
    C. A notebook.
    D. A pair of pajamas.

3. What could he not wait to do?

    A. Use his knapsack.
    B. Use his list.
    C. Use the articles in his bag.
    D. Use his sleeping bag.

4. Who made a check-list for Miguel?

    A. His father.
    B. His mother.
    C. His parents.
    D. His teacher.

Part B

5. What did Miguel do when he realized it was raining?

    A. He went back to bed.
    B. He applauded.
    C. He screamed.
    D. He laughed.

6. What did Miguel's father offer to do?

    A. Telephone the teacher.
    B. Telephone Miguel's friends.
    C. Take him to the camp.
    D. Take him to school.

7. Who answered the telephone?

    A. Miguel.
    B. Miguel's father.
    C. Miguel's mother.
    D. Miguel's teacher.

8. Why did Miguel applaud?

    A. He was happy to see his parents.
    B. He was happy that the rain had stopped.
    C. He could still go to camp.
    D. He was happy to see his teacher.

MIGUEL GOES TO CAMP

GENERAL QUESTIONS

Part A

1. Why was Miguel excited?

    A. He was going to leave home for the first time.
    B. He was going to be with his friends.
    C. He was going to his first camp that weekend.
    D. He was going to buy his first knapsack.

2. What did he do every night?

    A. Check to see what his mother had bought him.
    B. Check his list to see if he had everything.
    C. Check to see if everything was in the knapsack.
    D. Check to see if his knapsack was still there.

3. What did he begin to use?

    A. His sleeping bag.
    B. His checklist.
    C. His knapsack.
    D. His money.

4. Why did Miguel go to bed early on Thursday night?

    A. So he would wake up early on Friday morning.
    B. So that he would sleep well.
    C. Because he was going to see his teacher on Friday.
    D. Because he was tired.

Part B

5. What did Miguel realize when he awoke?

    A. He was late.
    B. He was not yet packed.
    C. It was raining heavily.
    D. It was drizzling.

6. Why did his parents run to his room?

    A. They had heard his knocks.
    B. They had heard his coughs.
    C. They had heard his screams
    D. They had seen the rain.

7. What happened while they were in Miguel's bedroom?

    A. His teacher came to their house.
    B. The telephone rang.
    C. The rain stopped.
    D. His father telephoned the teacher.

8. What did the teacher tell Miguel's father?

    A. To keep Miguel at home.
    B. To give Miguel his regards.
    C. To say that the camp was cancelled.
    D. To say that the camp would still be held.

ADOLFO'S BOOK

BASIC QUESTIONS

Part A

1. Which teacher recommended a book to the class?

    A. The literature teacher.
    B. The Cuban teacher.
    C. The anthology teacher.
    D. The history teacher.

2. Why did Adolfo go to the bookstore?

    A. To meet his friend.
    B. To see if he could find the book.
    C. To read the book.
    D. To speak to the owner of the store.

3. When did he go to the shopping centre?

    A. Next day.
    B. On Friday.
    C. After class.
    D. Before class.

4. What happened at the store in the shopping centre?

    A. Adolfo bought the book.
    B. Adolfo could not afford the price of the book.
    C. Adolfo did not like the book.
    D. Adolfo did not find the book.

Part B

5. What did he decide to do when he returned home?

    A. Show the book to his mother.
    B. Show the book to his father.
    C. Show the book to his brother.
    D. Show the book to his sister.

6. What did he do when he did not find the book?

    A. He went back to the store.
    B. He started to cry.
    C. He telephoned the bookstore.
    D. He called his mother.

7. Who took him back to the bookstore?

    A. His parents.
    B. His brother.
    C. His sister.
    D. His mother.

8. Who gave him his book at the bookstore?

    A. His friend.
    B. The owner of the store.
    C. His mother.
    D. The clerk in the store.

ADOLFO'S BOOK

GENERAL QUESTIONS

Part A

1. What did the teacher tell the class?

    A. To read a book.
    B. To buy a literature book.
    C. To buy a collection of Cuban accounts.
    D. To buy a collection of Cuban stories.

2. Where did Adolfo go?

    A. To a bookstore at his school.
    B. To a bookstore near his school.
    C. To a bookstore near his house.
    D To a bookstore in the shopping centre.

3. Why did he not buy the book he found there?

    A. It was too expensive.
    B. It was not the one he wanted.
    C. It was in a bad condition.
    D. It was not for sale.

4. What did he decide to do next?

    A. Go to a bookstore in the shopping centre.
    B. Go to the bookstore beside his house.
    C. Go to the library to look for the book.
    D. Go to a different shopping centre.

Part B

5. What happened when Adolfo opened his bag?

    A. He could not find the book.
    B. He could not find his money.
    C. He saw that his bag was empty.
    D. He saw that his book was there.

6. What did the manager tell him when he telephoned him?

    A. That he had not found his book.
    B. That he had found his book.
    C. That he had sold his book.
    D. That he had sent his book to him.

7. What did the manager tell Adolfo when he arrived at the store?

    A. That he could not find the book.
    B. That he was too busy to talk to him.
    C. That he did not remember speaking to him.
    D. That he had sent the book to him.

8. Why did Adolfo hug the store clerk?

    A. Because he knew who he was.
    B. Because he was happy to see him.
    C. Because he gave him his book.
    D. Because he bought the book for him.

ENRIQUE'S NIGHTMARE

BASIC QUESTIONS

Part A

1. What did Enrique see when he opened his eyes?

    A   Three strange objects in the room.
    B. Three persons in the room.
    C. Three round objects in the room.
    D. Three identical objects in the room.

2. What did he see to the right of the room?

    A. A vase with flowers and some cards.
    B. A table with flowers and some cards.
    C. A television and two armchairs.
    D. A television, an armchair and two small chairs.

3. What did he think when he could not get up?

    A. That he was tied to the bed.
    B. That he was badly hurt.
    C. That he was very ill.
    D. That he was in the hospital.

4. What did he do when he could not get up?

    A. He shouted to the nurse.
    B. He began to scream.
    C. He began to cry.
    D. He shouted for his mother.

Part B

5. Who heard Enrique's screams?

    A. His mother.
    B. His parents.
    C. The nurses.
    D. The nurse and doctor.

6. What did Enrique do when he got out of bed?

    A. He discussed his problem with his mother.
    B. He bathed and got dressed.
    C. He had breakfast and then got dressed.
    D. He bathed and had breakfast.

7. What was he going to do with his friends?

    A. Buy a new toy bicycle.
    B. Buy a new bicycle.
    C. Have a bicycle race.
    D. Have a bicycle sale with them.

8. Who was taking Enrique to the hospital?

    A. The rider of the bicycle with which he collided.
    B. His mother and his friends.
    C. His friends and their parents.
    D. The driver of the car with which he collided.

ENRIQUE'S NIGHTMARE

GENERAL QUESTIONS

Part A

1. What happened when Enrique opened his eyes?

    A. He could not see.
    B. He did not recognize the room.
    C. He was frightened.
    D. He became very ill.

2. What did he see to the left of the room?

    A. A vase with flowers and some cards.
    B. A television and two small chairs.
    C. A table with flowers and some cards.
    D. A television and an armchair.

3. What happened when he tried to get up?

    A. He could not do so.
    B. He fell out of bed.
    C. He hurt himself badly.
    D. He did it very easily.

4. Why did he begin to scream?

    A. He heard a frightening sound.
    B. He realized he was in the hospital.
    C. He heard the nurse's voice.
    D. He thought he was in hospital.

Part B

5. How did Enrique realize that he was dreaming?

    A. His mother awoke him and told him.
    B. He fell out of the chair.
    C. He saw himself in the mirror.
    D. He was very afraid.

6. What did he do after he bathed and got dressed?

    A. He went to the kitchen and hurriedly had breakfast.
    B. He went to the kitchen and prepared breakfast.
    C. He went to the kitchen and helped his mother.
    D. He went to the kitchen and told his mother to hurry.

7. What happened when he raced on to the street?

    A. He hit a chauffeur.
    B. He collided with a car.
    C. He made a sudden turn.
    D. He fell off the bicycle.

8. What did the driver do?

    A. Put Enrique back on his bicycle.
    B. Called his friends immediately.
    C. Put him in his car and took him to the hospital.
    D. Called his mother immediately.

A DAY IN THE PARK

BASIC QUESTIONS

Part A

1. Who did Rosario telephone?

    A. Her friend Carmen.
    B. Her father's friend.
    C. Her mother's friend.
    D. Her sister's friend.

2. What was being celebrated?

    A. Rosario's birthday.
    B. Rosario's father's birthday.
    C. Rosario's mother's birthday.
    D. Rosario's friend's birthday.

3. Who wanted to play baseball?

    A. Rosario and Carmen.
    B. Rosario's father.
    C. Rosario's mother
    D. Rosario's sister.

4. How many candles did Rosario put on the cake.

    A. Twenty.
    B. Thirty.
    C. Forty.
    D. Twenty-five.

Part B

5. Where did they take a walk after lunch?

    A. In the garden.
    B. In the picnic area.
    C. In the shade.
    D. In the pastures.

6. How were they feeling when they decided to leave?

    A. They were feeling happy.
    B. They were feeling tired.
    C. They were feeling hungry.
    D. They were feeling sad.

7. What were they looking for under the tree?

    A. Their basket.
    B. Their clothes.
    C. Their books.
    D. Their flowers.

8. How did they find it?

    A. A man gave it to them.
    B. Rosario saw it in the tree.
    C. A lady gave it to them.
    D. Rosario's father saw it in the tree.

A DAY IN THE PARK

GENERAL QUESTIONS

Part A

1. What did Rosario invite Carmen to do?

    A. Go to her house.
    B. Go on a picnic with her.
    C. Go to a party with her.
    D. Go to see her mother with her.

2. What did Rosario's father want to do?

    A. He wanted to eat.
    B. He wanted to rest.
    C. He wanted to play baseball.
    D. He wanted to take a walk.

3. What did they have to eat?

    A. Sandwiches, chicken, fruit and cake.
    B. Sandwiches, cake, wine and chicken.
    C. Chicken, fruit, cake, wine and sandwiches.
    D. Chicken, cake, wine and fruit.

4. What happened after Rosario put the candles on the cake?

    A. She could not find the matches.
    B. She lit them.
    C. She hugged her mother.
    D. She cut the cake.

Part B

5. What did they do after they ate?

    A. They picked some flowers in the garden.
    B. They went for a walk in the garden.
    C. They played "pass the ball" in the garden.
    D. They passed by the garden.

6. What happened when they decided to go home?

    A. They could not find their basket.
    B. They could not find Rosario.
    C. They could not find their way out.
    D. They could not find their favourite tree.

7. What did they hear when they decided to leave?

    A. The voice of a woman.
    B. The voice of a baby.
    C. The voice of Rosario.
    D. The voice of a man.

8. What did this person tell them?

    A. That they should leave immediately.
    B. That they should not leave.
    C. That he had their basket.
    D. That they had his basket.

ISABEL'S SURPRISE

BASIC QUESTIONS

Part A

1. With whom did Isabel go to the beauty salon?

    A. With her friend.
    B. With her mother.
    C. With her sister.
    D. With her teacher.

2. Why did they go to the beauty salon?

    A. They wanted to talk to the owner.
    B. They wanted to look pretty for a concert.
    C. They wanted to see the other clients.
    D. They wanted to see the inside of the beauty salon.

3. What did they want to do?

    A. Cut their hair.
    B. Paint their nails.
    C. Cut their hair and paint their nails.
    D. Cut their hair and nails.

4. What did the hairdresser say they would have to do?

    A. Wait.
    B. Leave.
    C. Cut off their hair.
    D. Cut their nails.

Part B

5. Why did they decide to leave the salon?

    A. It was very late.
    B. It was too crowded.
    C. They did not like the hairdresser.
    D. They did not like the salon.

6. What did they leave for the hairdresser?

    A. A note explaining why they had to leave.
    B. Money for her services.
    C. A note saying goodbye.
    D. Some information for clients.

7. Why did they take a taxi?

    A. They had missed the bus.
    B. They did not like the bus.
    C. They did not like the salon.
    D. They had missed the hairdresser.

8. Where did they go?

    A. To Marta's house.
    B. To Isabel's house.
    C. To the concert.
    D. To look for the hairdresser.

ISABEL'S SURPRISE

GENERAL QUESTIONS

Part A

1. Where did Isabel and Marta go?

    A. To Marta's house.
    B. To a beauty salon.
    C. To a concert.
    D. To an elegant store.

2. What were they going to do after that?

    A. Go to a party.
    B. Go to a concert.
    C. Visit their friend.
    D. Visit their clients.

3. When would the hairdresser attend to them?

    A. In five minutes' time.
    B. In an hour's time.
    C. When she had combed her hair.
    D. When she was finished with the other clients.

4. What did the girls decide to do?

    A. Wait.
    B. Leave.
    C. Call their parents.
    D. Call their friends.

Part B

5. Why did they call their parents?

    A. To ask their permission to go to a party.
    B. To ask their permission to change their hairstyles.
    C. To let them know where they were.
    D. To let them speak to the hairdresser.

6. What happened to them while they waited?

    A. They became nervous and anxious.
    B. They became tired.
    C. They became anxious.
    D. They became anxious and tired.

7. How long did they wait?

    A. One hour.
    B. Two hours.
    C. More than two and a half hours.
    D. Half an hour.

8. What did they discover at Isabel's house?

    A. That the night of the concert had passed.
    B. That they were mistaken about the date of the concert.
    C. That they were too late for the concert.
    D. That the concert would be on Thursday night.

A LATE ARRIVAL

BASIC QUESTIONS

Part A

1. When the alarm clock sounded the narrator…

    A. jumped out of bed.
    B. went back to sleep.
    C. was sweating and trembling.
    D. covered his head with the sheet.

2. What did the narrator feel like doing?

    A. Going back to sleep.
    B. Jumping out of bed.
    C. Going into his mother's bedroom.
    D. Putting the sheet on the bed.

3. Why did the narrator have to get up right away?

    A. His mother wanted to spread the bed.
    B. His breakfast was ready.
    C. He would be late.
    D. He had to go into his mother's room.

4. Why did the narrator run from the house?

    A. The bus he wanted had left him.
    B. His mother told him to run as it was 6 o'clock.
    C. He had spent too much time eating breakfast.
    D. He wanted to catch the 6 o'clock bus.

Part B

5. How long was the bus ride?

    A. Many hours.
    B. One hour.
    C. Fifty minutes.
    D. One hour and a quarter.

6. Why did the narrator start running?

    A. He wanted to arrive on time.
    B. He wanted to run for a long distance.
    C. He did not want the bus to disappear.
    D. He wanted to get to the bus.

7. The narrator did not know the time because…

    A. he had left his watch on the bus.
    B. he had forgotten his watch at home.
    C. the watch had stopped working.
    D. he was always unfortunate with his watch.

8. What did the narrator do when he reached his destination?

    A. He asked what time it was.
    B. He asked what he should do.
    C. He apologised for arriving late.
    D. He asked for the boss.

A LATE ARRIVAL

GENERAL QUESTIONS

Part A

1. How did the narrator get awake?

    A. His mother woke him.
    B. He heard a strange sound.
    C. The alarm clock rang.
    D. The bed was shaking.

2. The narrator's mother told him that…

    A. he could sleep for a few minutes more.
    B. he would have to run very fast.
    C. he had to leave the house immediately.
    D. he would be late and should get up immediately.

3. The narrator's mother…

    A. prepared his breakfast.
    B. covered him with the sheet.
    C. ran outside to stop the bus.
    D. went to her bedroom.

4. What did the narrator have for breakfast?

    A. Ham and eggs.
    B. Eggs and bread.
    C. Bread and jam.
    D. Ham and bread.

Part B

5. What did the narrator realise when he got off the bus?

    A. That he had arrived late.
    B. That he was on the wrong street.
    C. That he had a long distance to walk.
    D. That he had taken the wrong bus.

6. The narrator did not know…

    A. what time it was.
    B. where he was going.
    C. how long he should wait.
    D. where he had left his watch.

7. When the boss arrived, what did he say to the narrator?

    A. He asked why the narrator arrived late.
    B. He apologised for arriving late.
    C. He asked what time the narrator had arrived.
    D. He gave an excuse for his late arrival.

8. After speaking to the narrator, the boss…

    A. told him to start working.
    B. introduced the narrator to the other employees.
    C. told the employees about the late arrival.
    D. went away for an hour and a half.

A VALUABLE LESSON

BASIC QUESTIONS

Part A

1. Where was the narrator born?

    A. In a small town.
    B. In Kingston.
    C. Near the primary school.
    D. On a farm.

2. The narrator did not go to secondary school because…

    A. his brothers and sisters had to go.
    B. his parents could not afford it.
    C. he had to sell vegetables.
    D. he was living in Kingston.

3. What did the children do on the farm?

    A. They did their school work.
    B. They set up a big market
    C. They had a good time.
    D. They planted vegetables.

4. The narrator's mother…

    A. went to Kingston to live.
    B. cultivated vegetables on the farm.
    C. went to market to sell vegetables.
    D. took vegetables to the secondary school.

Part B

5. What did the narrator do in the market?

    A   He bought vegetables from a man.
    B. He helped his mother to sell.
    C. He marked the price of the vegetables.
    D. He spent time speaking to the buyers.

6. What did the narrator learn after some years had passed?

    A. To dress and speak well.
    B. That it was important to arrive on time.
    C. What he had to do to graduate.
    D. That too many years had passed for him to graduate.

7. What had happened to the narrator's family after some years?

    A. They also moved to Kingston.
    B. Life had improved for them.
    C. They still lived in the country.
    D. They moved to a better town.

8. What lesson did the narrator learn?

    A   That money was very important.
    B. That his parents should be invited to the activities.
    C. That he was really proud of his family.
    D. That he would receive a present.

A VALUABLE LESSON

GENERAL QUESTIONS

Part A

1. The narrator was born...

    A. in Kingston.
    B. near the primary school.
    C. on a farm.
    D. in a small town.

2. Why could the narrator go only to primary school?

    A. The secondary school was too far.
    B. His parents had enough money so he did not have to s\: more.
    C. His parents felt that secondary education was unneces\:
    D. His parents could not afford to send him.

3. The children had to...

    A. do their school work.
    B. go to market.
    C. work and plant vegetables.
    D. sell vegetables.

4. Why did the narrator's mother go to Kingston?

    A. To live there.
    B. To sell vegetables.
    C. To cultivate vegetables.
    D. To take the narrator to school.

Part B

5. The man who bought vegetables from the narrator's mother offered to…

    A. buy more vegetables.
    B. take the mother to meet his family.
    C. pay for the narrator's secondary education.
    D. take them back to the country.

6. Where would the narrator live?

    A. In an academic institution.
    B. With the man's family.
    C. With his parents.
    D. At the secondary school.

7. The narrator did not want to invite his parents to his graduation because…

    A. they lived far away in the country.
    B. he believed his parents did not have the money to come to Kingston.
    C. he thought his friends would not accept his parents.
    D. he thought his friends would reject him once they met his parents.

8. What happened after the graduation?

    A. There were many activities.
    B. Many presentations were made.
    C. The narrator was congratulated by his parents.
    D. The narrator's father wished him a Merry Christmas.

A DISAPPOINTING TRIP

BASIC QUESTIONS

Part A

1. Where were the students going?

    A. To a camp.
    B. To the San Martin School.
    C. To meet some young people.
    D. To the country.

2. The students were going to...

    A. prepare a meal.
    B. learn some Geography from the teacher.
    C. climb a mountain.
    D. study a map of the region.

3. Why was the teacher a good guide?

    A. She knew the place and had climbed that mountain.
    B. She had gone on excursions many times.
    C. She was well-known in the area.
    D. She liked excursions.

4. What did the teacher realize?

    A. That she had not counted the students.
    B. That everything was all right.
    C. That a student was missing.
    D. That some students were falling behind.

Part B

5. What did they hear in the bushes?

    A. A roaring sound.
    B. Singing.
    C. Crying.
    D. A loud noise.

6. What had happened?

    A. A boy had run away.
    B. A boy had hurt himself.
    C. A stone had fallen on the boy.
    D. The boy had tried to walk too far.

7. When the boy called out…

    A. his companions came.
    B. the teacher came.
    C. nobody replied.
    D. he felt more pain.

8. Where was the boy taken by his friends?

    A. To the top of the mountain.
    B. To a place where he could lie down.
    C. To the foot of the mountain.
    D. To the hospital.

A DISAPPOINTING TRIP

GENERAL QUESTIONS

Part A

1. When the students set out they felt...

   A. that it was too early.
   B. very excited.
   C. that the mountain was too high.
   D. that they should have left at 5 o'clock.

2. Why did the Geography teacher go with the students?

   A. She had a good map of the area.
   B. It was a Geography trip.
   C. She liked to go on trips.
   D. She liked the food they were taking.

3. The Geography teacher was going as a guide because she...

   A. always enjoyed excursions.
   B. had climbed various mountains.
   C. knew the place and had climbed that mountain.
   D. was from that area.

4. When the student was discovered missing, the teacher...

   A. decided to return home immediately.
   B. sent the students ahead.
   C. tried to find out what had happened.
   D. decided to search for him.

Part B

5. What did the students discover in the bushes?

    A. That the boy was getting attention.
    B. That the boy was still crying.
    C. That the missing boy was there.
    D. That the boy had been searching for something.

6. Where did the boy feel pain?

    A. In the area under his shirt.
    B. In his back.
    C. In his leg and head.
    D. In his right leg.

7. What was the result of the fall?

    A. The boy's leg was cut.
    B. The boy could only walk a short distance.
    C. The boy's shirt was torn.
    D. The boy became unconscious.

8. What did the boy try to do but could not?

    A. Reply to the shouts he heard.
    B. Call out to someone.
    C. Get up and walk.
    D. Look for his friends.

A SURPRISING MOVIE

BASIC QUESTIONS

Part A

1. When did the narrator go to bed?

    A. At about 8 o'clock.
    B. At 6 o'clock.
    C. At 10 o'clock.
    D. At midnight.

2. What did the narrator do until late?

    A. He went to the movies.
    B. He looked at a film at home.
    C. He went shopping with his father.
    D. He visited another little boy.

3. What happened to the little boy in the movie?

    A. He got lost while shopping with his father.
    B. He went to see his father.
    C. He bought something for his father.
    D. He went visiting with his father.

4. Why did the little boy leave his father?

    A. He wanted to speak to a guard.
    B. He wanted to play with a friend.
    C. He wanted to find the Toy Department.
    D. He wanted to get some help.

Part B

5. Why was the father frantic?

   A. Because the boy was playing with toys.
   B. Because he wanted to see a movie.
   C. Because he could not find his son.
   D. Because the guard did not help him.

6. What did the boy do in the cafeteria?

   A. He bought cakes and sandwiches.
   B. He ate cakes and then paid for them.
   C. He did not pay for what he ate.
   D. He asked a guard to pay for the cakes.

7. How did the father find out what had happened?

   A. He saw his son and spoke to him.
   B. He asked the lady in the cafeteria.
   C. He asked the guard.
   D. The people in the Toy Department told him.

8. What happened two years before?

   A. The narrator and his father had an accident.
   B. The narrator left his father in a store.
   C. The narrator had an experience similar to the one in the movie.
   D. The narrator celebrated his second birthday.

A SURPRISING MOVIE

GENERAL QUESTIONS

Part A

1. Why was the narrator awake until late?

    A. He was eight years old on that day.
    B. His friend was visiting him.
    C. He looked at a movie.
    D. He went out with his father.

2. The father went shopping and…

    A. bought a tie.
    B. selected some toys.
    C. chose a suit and some ties.
    D. bought some clothes.

3. What did the little boy do while his father was shopping?

    A. He left the store.
    B. He waited for 2 hours.
    C. He went to the Toy Department.
    D. He went to look for a guard.

4. Why did the father need help?

    A. He had a problem with the guards.
    B. He could not find his son.
    C. He could not decide what to buy.
    D. He could not find the Toy Department.

Part B

5. The little boy was having a good time because...

    A. he was with his father.
    B. he was playing with toys.
    C. his father bought him a remote control car.
    D. he went for a train ride.

6. What did the guard in the cafeteria do?

    A. He paid for the food the boy ate.
    B. He put the boy outside.
    C. He took the boy to his father.
    D. He took the boy to the Toy Department.

7. What did the father ask the guard?

    A. If he knew what had happened.
    B. If his son was in the cafeteria.
    C. If he had seen his son.
    D. If his son had bought food in the cafeteria.

8. Why was the movie surprising to the narrator?

    A. His father looked like the father in the movie.
    B. The end was not what he expected.
    C. He had a big surprise when he went shopping.
    D. The same thing had happened to him.

THE MISSING BAG

BASIC QUESTIONS

Part A

1. The eight people had been friends since they...

    A. first met in a restaurant.
    B. became successful.
    C. established their business.
    D. were in primary school.

2. Why were the friends meeting?

    A. They were celebrating their success.
    B. They wanted to start a business together.
    C. They had just graduated from primary school.
    D. They always laughed when they were together.

3. What did Marta suddenly say to her friends?

    A. That she was sorry she had come.
    B. That she had found a lot of money.
    C. That she could not find her bag.
    D. That she had counted the money.

4. Where was Marta's money?

    A. She had left it at home.
    B. It was in the bag.
    C. She had given it to a friend.
    D. She had used it to pay the bill.

Part B

5. What did Marta ask her friends to do?

    A. Pay for another bag.
    B. Leave the restaurant.
    C. Give her some money.
    D. Help her to look for the bag.

6. Why were Marta's friends upset?

    A. Because she was crying.
    B. Because they could not get to eat.
    C. Because they wanted to talk.
    D. Because they could not find her anywhere.

7. What had happened to Marta's bag?

    A. She had brought it to the restaurant.
    B. She had given it to a man to keep for her.
    C. She had left it in a taxi.
    D. She had put it on her seat.

8. Why did Marta give the man money?

    A. She had forgotten to pay her taxi fare.
    B. She wanted to reward him for being honest.
    C. She owed him $500.
    D. She was pleased with the ride in the taxi.

THE MISSING BAG

GENERAL QUESTIONS

Part A

1. When did the friends meet each other for the first time?

    A. When they set up a business together.
    B. When they were in a restaurant.
    C. When they became successful.
    D. When they were in primary school.

2. The reason for the meeting was that the friends ...

    A. were hungry and wanted to eat.
    B. had just left school.
    C. wanted to have a good time together.
    D. planned to set up a business together.

3. Marta was very sure that...

    A. she had entered the restaurant on time.
    B. the restaurant was good.
    C. the bag was left in the restaurant.
    D. she had the bag when she entered the restaurant.

4. What was Marta wondering?

    A. If she should ask the waiter about the bag.
    B. If her camera was in the bag.
    C. If the bag had been stolen.
    D. If her friends would question her about the bag.

40

Part B

5. Marta asked her friends to ...

    A. help her look for the bag.
    B. give her some money.
    C. pay for the meal.
    D. pay for another bag.

6. The man who came into the room said that...

    A. the seat of his taxi had been damaged by a woman.
    B. a woman who had taken his taxi had not paid him.
    C. a woman had left a bag in his taxi.
    D. trash had been left on the seat of his taxi.

7. Why had the man come to the restaurant?

    A. He discovered the damage to his car.
    B. He thought the woman might need her bag.
    C. He wanted to eat in that restaurant.
    D. He wanted to find the woman as quickly as possible.

8. What did Marta's friends do?

    A. They explained to her that they had to leave.
    B. They paid the bill of $500.
    C. They left the restaurant without speaking to Marta.
    D. They said goodbye to Marta and left without explaining why.

SITUATIONS

BASIC AND GENERAL PROFICIENCY

COMMON SECTION

Candidates are required to write short responses in Spanish to a series of situations described in English.

This section corresponds to **Paper 2, Section 1 and is worth 20 marks**.

BASIC AND GENERAL PROFICIENCY

SITUATIONS

Write in SPANISH the information required by each of the situations given below. **Do not use more than one sentence for each situation**. DO NOT translate the situations given.

1. You are leaving home on an exchange programme to a Spanish-speaking country. Write the note which your sister leaves on your bed with a suggestion for improving your Spanish.

2. Your mother has written strict instructions about an electrical appliance which she recently bought. Write one of the instructions.

3. A nurse at the hospital where you are visiting your sick friend allows you to see him but before doing so, she shows you the note of caution which was written by his doctor. Write the note.

4. You have a part-time job but you cannot come to work this week. Write a message to your boss saying why you will be absent.

5. You are in a restaurant waiting on a friend who is an hour late and you decide to leave. Write a message, which you leave with the waiter, apologising for not being there.

6. While your parents are on vacation in Mexico you become involved in something that occupies a lot of your time. Write a telegram to your parents explaining why you cannot meet them at the airport.

7. You were the victim of a robbery a week ago and the Police need you to come to the station immediately to identify the robber. Leave a note for your parents telling them that you will soon return.

8. Your parents told you to stay at home but you suddenly develop severe pains in your stomach and decide to seek help. Write a message to your parents saying where you have gone.

9. You go to your friend's house to discuss a matter with him but he has gone out. Leave a message for him telling him why you came by.

10. You have spent all your pocket money and want to go to the movies. Write a message to your brother explaining why you have borrowed some of his money.

11. You have an evening job as a receptionist in a hotel and a gentleman phones to make a reservation. Write a message to the Supervisor explaining the arrangements you made.

12. You return home from school on your birthday and see a gift from your parents but you have arranged to go out with your friends. Write a message to your parents thanking them for their kindness.

13. You want to cancel your arrangements to see your boyfriend next week because something has come up. Write a message to your boyfriend apologising for the change of plans.

14. A passenger in front of you wants to know how the old lady next to him would react to his smoking but discovers that she is deaf. Write the note which he shows her in an effort to find this out.

15. You have decided to participate in an activity which is being planned by a club in your community but your mother is not in favour of this. Write the note which she leaves for you to warn you of the risks involved.

16. Your little cousin has been trying to complete a task for the past two weeks and telephones to ask for you while you are out. Write the message which your brother takes.

17. A girlfriend has just had her hair done. Write a message to her in class saying what you think of her new hairstyle.

18. You agreed to help a classmate with an assignment. Pass a note to your classmate giving a reason for changing your mind.

19. You have just received an unexpected invitation to a party but have nothing suitable to wear. Write a note in which you ask your sister, who will return home while you are out, to lend you her new dress.

20. Your father is giving a speech at his Company's Award Ceremony and the guests are falling asleep. Write a note to your father suggesting that he should stop talking.

21. Your teacher has asked you to give a book to a student in another class but you understand that he has left the school. Leave a note for your teacher in which you provide her with his new address.

22. You have house guests for whom you leave a special instruction in the bathroom. Write the instruction.

23. You are leaving home without seeing your mother before you leave for the airport. Write the good-bye note which you leave for her.

24. While your family is visiting friends, your brother is being impossible. Write the note in which you tell him to conduct himself properly.

25. You need to speak to your pastor but he is not in his office when you get there. Write a message in which you tell him what you want to talk to him about.

26. Your mother sends you with a note in which she apologises to her friend for not being able to meet her at the airport. Write the note.

27. Your father is unable to go to work and sends you to his colleague with a special request. Write the request.

28. You are at a concert with your girlfriend who did not hear something that was said by the Master of Ceremonies. Write the note which she passes to you to query the statement.

29. While you were out your brother wanted your opinion on something. Write the note which he leaves for you.

30. Your friend passes you a note during class time asking you to explain a word. Write a note in which you tell her you are not able to do so.

31. Your aunt has had an accident. Write the note you send to convey your sympathy to her.

32. Your cousin has just been successful in his exams. Write the congratulatory note which you send him.

33. You are unable to attend classes and send an excuse to your teacher with a friend explaining the reason for your absence. Write the excuse.

34. You are on vacation and arrive at a hotel to check in but there is no one at the desk to receive you. You leave your luggage and a note for the receptionist. Write the note.

35. You have been awaiting the arrival of a friend but have to leave home suddenly. Write the note which you leave for him to explain your absence.

36. Your parents expect you home at a certain time but you will be late. Write a note which you send with your friend to explain the reason you will not be home on time.

37. Your aunt has sent you a lovely gift for your birthday. Write a note to thank her.

38. You are giving a party at your home on Saturday. Write the note which you send to your friends to invite them to the party.

39. You go to your friend's house to tell her about your recent trip abroad but she is not there. Write the note you leave to describe your trip.

40. While your mother is out, an old friend of hers stops by to see her. Write the note which she leaves with you expressing her disappointment.

41. Your sister has an urgent problem and wants you to phone your mother at work. Write the message she gives you to tell your mother.

42. You and your classmate have different opinions as to which team will win a sporting event tomorrow. Write your classmate's prediction of the outcome of the event.

43. You need a book from the nearby library but do not have time to get it, so you ask your brother to get it for you. Write the note which you give to him to take to the librarian requesting her help in finding the book.

44. Your classmate is planning to visit your home. Write a note in which you tell him what time is convenient for him to do so.

45. During a shopping trip you were assisted by a very friendly attendant. Write a note in which you express your appreciation to him/her.

46. You go to your aunt's office to discuss a matter with her but she is not there. Write a note to her informing her that you had come and explaining why you wanted to see her.

47. Your sister is going to visit your grandmother but you are unable to go. Write a message which you send promising to visit at another time.

48. Your friends are visiting your church for the first time. Write a note telling them where it is located.

49. Your parents have decided to punish your little brother for something which he did at school, but you believe that the punishment is too harsh. Write a note to your parents expressing your disagreement with their decision.

50. Your brother has promised to visit your friend in Venezuela while he is travelling there. Write a note to your friend in which you introduce your brother to him/her.

51. You have recommended your dressmaker/tailor to your friend. Write a note confirming that you recommended him/her.

52. You ask your sister to return something which you bought at a store and later discovered was damaged. Write a note which you give to her to take to the store.

53. The manager of the store where you have applied for a job sends a message to you concerning the outcome of your application. Write the message.

54. An exchange student at your school accepts your invitation to go to a place of interest but she has to go somewhere else first. Write the note she gives you to remind you of where to pick her up.

55. Your new neighbour asks you to attend his birthday party but you do not accept the invitation. Write the note you receive from him persuading you to attend.

56. You went to the flower shop to buy flowers for your grandmother for a special occasion. Write the message which you want to accompany the flowers.

57. Your friend has a tragedy in her family. Write a note in which you offer your help.

58. You do not approve of something your sister has done. Write a note to her expressing your disapproval.

59. You want to avoid discussing a matter with your brother. Write a note to him expressing your disagreement with his views.

60. You doubt very much that your friend's involvement in a particular concert is a good idea. Write a note expressing your doubts to her.

61. You have just listened to a very controversial discussion between your brother and his friends. You do not want to become involved but you later leave him a note expressing your personal view on the matter. Write the note.

62. You have received an invitation to a function which you are unable to attend. Write a note in which you express your regrets.

63. Your friend has been kind enough to do a big favour for you. Write a note to thank him.

64. Your mother is visiting your aunt whom you have not seen in many years. Write a note to your aunt expressing your best wishes to her.

65. It is your father's birthday. Write a message to him expressing your good wishes.

66. A student who has been unfriendly to you in the past, sends you a note in class indicating a change of attitude. Write the note you receive.

67. Your younger brother has been very worried lately. Write the note he sends you asking for advice.

68. You want to miss a basketball match on Wednesday and send a message to the coach. Write the message he sends you telling you why you have to play.

69. Your friend's mother is ill and you send a note to her to express your wishes for a quick recovery. Write the note.

70. Your cousin in Trinidad has an important examination to sit. Write a note to express your hope that he/she will be successful.

71. Your parents have decided to punish you for taking the car without permission. Write a note to them to explain why you did this.

72. You would like the bookstore in town to order a special book for you. Write the note which you send to the manager.

73. You are thinking of doing a Summer Course abroad. Write a note to your teacher asking for advice on the matter.

74. You think your friend spends her money unwisely. Write a note to warn her about this matter.

75. Your friend is not speaking to you because she is upset that you have purchased the prettier of two things which you both bought. Write a note in which you compare both things favourably.

76. You learn that your friend who lives in Canada is in your country for a few days. He is not at his hotel when you go to see him. Write a note offering to show him around.

77. You would like to get your mother's opinion on a matter but she is not at home and you have to leave. Write the note which you leave, requesting her opinion.

78. Your aunt has written to tell you to choose one of two things which she is thinking of buying for you. Write a note to her expressing your preference.

79. You decided not to be involved in any of the co-curricular activities in your school. Write the note you receive from the president of one of the clubs, telling you the advantages of joining her club.

80. Your teacher invites someone to address your class. During the address she sends a message to you telling you that she wants you to do something. Write the message you receive from your teacher.

81. While you are not at home a phone call comes for you from abroad. Write the message that your father leaves for you, telling you what the caller said.

82. You feel very certain about a situation which your teacher is questioning. Write a note to her expressing this certainty.

83. You send a Christmas card to your sister who is abroad studying. Write the greetings which you send.

84. Your Spanish teacher has recently got married. Write a congratulatory note which you give to her in the Spanish class.

85. Your younger brother has a serious difficulty with a certain situation. Write a note in which you suggest a solution.

86. You have been invited to a special birthday celebration for your friend's father. Write the note of acceptance which you send to her mother.

87. A friend who has migrated writes you a letter. Write the first line of the letter which you send to your friend, telling him/her how happy you were to receive his/her letter.

88. You have been grounded by your parents for failing to observe a family rule. Write a note apologising for your mistake.

89. You have been invited to a special function but need to have more information about it. Write a brief note to the organizers requesting information about the dress code and the length of the function.

90. You have just returned from your cousin's home where you spent a week. Write a note in which you tell him/her what you enjoyed most about the visit.

91. You want your brother to do a favour for you. Write the note which you leave for him, promising him to return the favour.

92. You are at your best friend's house and his mother passes you a note requesting your help in planning a surprise party for your friend. Write the note.

93. Your older brother does not want anyone to enter his room when he is not there. Write the notice he puts on his door explaining the reason for his position.

94. A Venezuelan student has recently started attending your school. You receive a note from her requesting your help to improve her English. Write the note.

95. Your friends invite you to go to the movies with them, but your parents are not at home to give you permission. Write the note which you leave for them, telling them how much time you will spend there.

96. You spent a weekend with your friend in another town. Write a note to him/her telling him/her how you felt about the visit.

97. Your friend is leaving to study abroad. Write a note which you give him at the airport wishing him success and best wishes.

98. You were punished by your parents for being rude to one of their friends. Write a note to them telling them what lesson you learned from this.

99. Your friend has just passed her CXC Spanish Examination. Write a brief note telling her how you think this will help in the future.

100. Your mother is not at home when you return from school but she has left a note instructing you to do a special chore. Write the note.

LETTERS/DIALOGUES/COMPOSITIONS

GENERAL PROFICIENCY

This section corresponds to
Paper 2, Section 2 and is worth 30 marks

LETTERS

Write a letter in SPANISH of 130-150 words AND NO MORE. Use the tense or tenses appropriate to the topic.

1. You want a summer job in a Spanish-speaking country. Write a letter to the manager of a store you have heard about and include

    (i) personal information about yourself
    (ii) your reasons for wanting the job
    (iii) experience you have had in a similar position
    (iv) your travel plans.

2. A friend of yours wants to spend his/her holidays in the Spanish-speaking country you visited last year. Write a letter to your host family and mention

    (i) information about your friend
    (ii) why your friend wants to spend summer there
    (iii) suggestions for activities that would interest your friend
    (iv) some changes in the living arrangements that would make your friend more comfortable.

3. You arranged to spend three months with a family in a Spanish-speaking country. You are unhappy there and want to return home. Write a letter to your hosts and include

    (i) the reasons for your unhappiness
    (ii) your appreciation of their efforts to make you comfortable
    (iii) the travel arrangements for your return
    (iv) how you will spend your time when you return home.

4. You are working part-time in a hotel. Write a reply to a letter from someone in a Spanish-speaking country who has requested information about a holiday in your country. Include

    (i) some information about the hotel
    (ii) the attractions that are nearby
    (iii) some of the tours that are available
    (iv) an offer to provide additional information.

5. You are on an exchange programme in a Spanish-speaking country. Write a letter to your sister who is also studying Spanish and mention

    (i) your lost luggage
    (ii) the help you received from your host family
    (iii) what you bought when you went shopping
    (iv) how much you miss your family and friends.

6. You are planning to return to the Spanish-speaking country you visited last year. Write a letter to your friend in that country. Include

    (i) your reasons for returning
    (ii) details about your arrival
    (iii) suggestions as to what you want to do this time
    (iv) greetings to other friends.

7. Your parents have agreed that you can complete High School in a Spanish-speaking country. Write a letter to the Principal of the High School of your choice and mention

    (i) why you want to study there
    (ii) your academic achievements
    (iii) your extra-curricular interests
    (iv) when you wish to attend.

8. You have just bought a new pet which you are enjoying very much. Write a letter to your friend in a Spanish-speaking country telling him/her

    (i) what kind of pet you have bought
    (ii) what your family thinks of it
    (iii) how you take care of your pet
    (iv) your hope that he/she will see it one day.

9. Your father has just got a new job and your family will be in a Spanish-speaking country for one year. Write a letter to your friend in that country in which you

    (i) tell him/her the news
    (ii) explain what your father will be doing there
    (iii) say what you are looking forward to seeing
    (iv) express your hope to spend some time with him/her.

10. Your cousin who lives in a Spanish-speaking country has sent a ticket for you to spend the Summer holidays with him/her. Write a letter in which you

    (i) thank him/her for the kindness
    (ii) express your happiness
    (iii) tell him/her some of the things you want to do when you get there
    (iv) express your hope to see him/her soon.

11. You have just had a short story published in the newspaper. Write a letter to your former Spanish teacher who is studying in a Spanish-speaking country and

    (i) tell him/her the good news
    (ii) describe what the story is about
    (iii) say whether or not you plan to write more stories in the future
    (iv) promise to send him/her a copy.

12. Your penpal who lives in a Spanish-speaking country writes to tell you that he/she was placed first in the end of year examinations in school. Write a letter in which you

   (i)   congratulate him/her
   (ii) ask for more information about the examinations
   (iii) tell him/her how you feel about examinations
   (iv) wish him/her success in future examinations.

DIALOGUES

Write a dialogue in SPANISH of 130-150 words AND NO MORE. Use the tense or tenses appropriate to the topic.

1. You visit your Spanish-speaking friend who wants you to accompany her shopping. Write a dialogue between your friend and yourself in which you

    (i) exchange greetings
    (ii) discuss where you would be going
    (iii) talk about why you are unable to go
    (iv) arrange to go shopping on the following day.

2. You are visiting a Spanish-speaking country and the group leader is annoyed because you have not completed the chores assigned to you. Write a dialogue between you and your leader in which you

    (i) discuss the reasons for the problem
    (ii) talk about the attitude of children nowadays
    (iii) arrange a new time for doing the chores
    (iv) agree on a suitable punishment.

3. While on vacation in a Spanish-speaking country you witness the robbery of a store and so the police want to question you. Write a dialogue between a police officer and yourself in which you

    (i) arrange to go to the police station
    (ii) arrive at a description of the robber
    (iii) discuss the reward
    (iv) agree to continue the conversation on the following day.

4. You are in a Spanish-speaking country and go to a restaurant. You are not satisfied with the meal. Write a dialogue between yourself and the waiter in which you

    (i) exchange greetings
    (ii) agree on the dishes to be served
    (iii) discuss the problems with the meal
    (iv) agree on other dishes from the menu.

5. Your family is spending a year in a Spanish-speaking country. You and brother are planning a surprise party for one of your friends. Write a dialogue between you and your brother in which you

    (i) discuss what food will be served
    (ii) agree on the number of people to invite
    (iii) allocate responsibilities
    (iv) arrange a follow-up meeting.

6. You have been accepted into a High School in a Spanish-speaking country. Write a dialogue between yourself and your new Principal in which you

    (i) exchange greetings
    (ii) talk about the problems that could arise
    (iii) discuss the school rules
    (iv) arrange to meet some of the other students.

7. You are doing a course in a Spanish-speaking country and your teacher is annoyed because you have not submitted your Home Work assignment. He sends you to the Principal. Write a dialogue between yourself and the Principal in which you

    (i) discuss the reasons for the problem
    (ii) agree on a new date for submitting the assignment
    (iii) discuss a suitable punishment
    (iv) say goodbye to each other.

8. You are studying in a Spanish-speaking country and are about to graduate. Write a dialogue between yourself and a classmate in which you

    (i) talk about what you will wear
    (ii) discuss who will escort you
    (iii) talk about the dinner that has been planned
    (iv) discuss the advantages of going as a group.

9. You are attending school in a Spanish-speaking country and have a Science project. Write a dialogue between yourself and the School Librarian in which you

    (i) greet each other and discuss your needs
    (ii) discuss what the project is about
    (iii) arrange to use the book for longer than the usual time
    (iv) agree to take good care of the book.

10. You are an exchange student at a school in a Spanish-speaking country. You meet another student who is on a similar programme. Write a dialogue in which you

    (i) greet each other
    (ii) introduce yourselves
    (iii) talk about your respective countries
    (iv) promise to become friends and help each other.

11. While you are in the departure lounge of the airport on your way to a Spanish-speaking country, you see a Spanish-speaking friend whom you have not seen for some time. Write a dialogue in which you

    (i) express your happiness at seeing each other
    (ii) say why you are travelling
    (iii) discuss your destinations
    (iv) make arrangements to meet when you return.

12. Your Spanish-speaking friend is attending his/her first meeting at a Church of which you are a member. Write a dialogue in which you

    (i) greet each other
    (ii) discuss some of the activities which take place during the meetings
    (iii) talk about the plans for the Church's summer camp
    (iv) discuss some of the characteristics of the Church.

COMPOSITIONS

Write a composition in SPANISH of 130-150 words AND NO MORE. Use the tense or tenses appropriate to the topic.

1. You spent your summer holidays in a Spanish-speaking country. Write a composition in which you mention

    (i) the reasons you chose that country
    (ii) some of the places you visited
    (iii) an embarrassing incident in which you were involved
    (iv) what you liked most about the people.

2. During your stay in a Spanish-speaking country you plan a surprise birthday party for your room-mate. Write a composition describing

    (i) the arrangements you made to get your room-mate out of the house
    (ii) the food and drinks you prepared for the party
    (iii) the reaction of your room-mate on returning home
    (iv) the fun you had.

3. While vacationing in a Spanish-speaking country you rented a car and were involved in an accident. Describe

    (i) the village you were driving through
    (ii) what caused the accident
    (iii) the help you received from other drivers
    (iv) the drive to the hospital in the ambulance.

4. You spent a weekend in a Spanish-speaking country. Write a composition and describe

    (i) your arrival at the airport in that country
    (ii) a delicious meal you had
    (iii) some gifts that you bought
    (iv) what you enjoyed most about the trip.

5. While visiting a Spanish-speaking country, you and your friends went by train to another city. Write a composition and describe

    (i) your late arrival at the train station
    (ii) the group activities on the train
    (iii) an unexpected stop
    (iv) how you felt when you reached your destination.

6. You are studying in a Spanish-speaking country. Your teacher tells you to write a composition about life in your country and to describe

   (i) your family
   (ii) a typical dish
   (iii) some of the recreational activities
   (iv) some places of interest.

7. You have been chosen to do a presentation about your school to some Spanish-speaking exchange students. Write a composition in which you include

   (i) the name and size of your school
   (ii) the history of your school
   (iii) some of the clubs and extra-curricular activities
   (iv) what you like most about your school.

8. While you are on holidays in a Spanish-speaking country, you are asked to speak about your favourite tourist attraction in your country. Write a composition in which you include

   (i) the name and location of the place
   (ii) a description of the place
   (iii) how often you visit it
   (iv) what you like most about the place.

9. While you are vacationing in a Spanish-speaking country, you have been asked to speak about a camp you recently attended. Write a composition in which you include

   (i) the reason you attended the camp
   (ii) some of the activities which took place during the camp
   (iii) the most exciting day of the camp
   (iv) what you liked most about the camp.

10. While you are attending school in a Spanish-speaking country you enter a competition in which you must describe your neighbourhood. Write a composition in which you describe

    (i) the location of your neighbourhood
    (ii) what the public service facilities are like
    (iii) what the people are like
    (iv) some outstanding features of the neighbourhood.

11. Your family is living in a Spanish-speaking country for a year and your father has been involved in an accident to which you were a witness. Write a composition about

    (i) the vehicles which were involved in the accident
    (ii) the time the accident occurred
    (iii) what your father was doing when it happened
    (iv) the results of the accident.

12. You have just returned from a visit to a Spanish-speaking country. Write a composition in which you

    (i) explain the reason for your trip
    (ii) describe the persons who accompanied you
    (iii) tell about a well-known tourist attraction there
    (iv) relate an incident in the airport when you were returning.

READING COMPREHENSION

BASIC PROFICIENCY

Candidates are required to answer questions based on a variety of written material or graphic stimulus, for example, a continuous passage or an advertisement.

Questions will be in English and candidates are to write their answers in English. This section corresponds to **Paper 2, Section 4 and is worth 15 marks**.

Read the following carefully. DO NOT translate but answer the questions in ENGLISH.

PERSONAL DOMÉSTICO
EMBAJADA

Necesitamos una persona que tenga experiencia en trabajos domésticos, debe saber atender una mesa y reglas de etiqueta. Buen sueldo, dormir dentro, posibilidad de viajar. Si tienes experiencia comprobable pedir cita por el teléfono 261 0633, horas de oficina.

---

1. What does the applicant need to know?
2. What type of job is this?
3. What is said about accommodation?
4. What kind of experience should the applicant have?
5. How does an interested person apply?

Read the following carefully. DO NOT translate but answer the questions in ENGLISH.

MANTENIMIENTO

IMPERMEABLES PATO

- **LAVAR EN AGUA FRÍA CON JABÓN NEUTRO, AYUDANDO CON UNA ESPONJA.**
- **NO PLANCHAR.**
- **NO USAR NUNCA ACETONA NI ALCOHOL.**
- **DEBE EVITARSE EL CONTACTO CON OBJETOS CALIENTES.**

1. What item of clothing is this label from?
2. What should be used to help with washing?
3. What should not be done after washing?
4. What objects should be avoided.
5. Why is alcohol mentioned?

Read the following carefully. DO NOT translate but answer the questions in ENGLISH.

1. What are two (2) conditions that ZQ9 is supposed to cure?
2. In what form is the medication?
3. Where is it usually available for sale?
4. If it is not where it usually is, what can the interested person do?
5. What season of the year is the need for ZQ9 most likely to occur?

Read the following carefully. DO NOT translate but answer the questions in ENGLISH.

1. What is Pajarito invited to do?
2. Who is inviting him?
3. What happens during the meetings?
4. Why is Pajarito concerned?
5. What explanation is he given?

Read the following carefully. DO NOT translate but answer the questions in ENGLISH.

Roberto está muy contento hoy porque su mamá le va a llevar a visitar a su tía en la ciudad. A Roberto le gusta mucho la casa de su tía. Es muy grande, cómoda y bonita. La tía Elena tiene muchos muebles antiguos que pertenecían a sus padres. El mecedor del bisabuelo es la pieza especial de Roberto.

Cada vez que Roberto visita a la tía Elena ella le prepara todos los postres favoritos - helados caseros, quesillo, pastel de chocolate y flan. La mamá de Roberto siempre le dice que la tía le mima demasiado porque además de darle la comida que le encanta, ella le compra ropa, y juegos para su computadora.

¡Qué tiempo maravilloso voy a tener! piensa Roberto.

1. Why is Roberto happy? (2)
2. What does he like? (1)
3. Why does he like it? (2)
4. What is to be found there? (1)
5. Who used to own these things? (1)
6. Describe them. (2)
7. Who owned the piece which is Roberto's favourite? (1)
8. What happens when Roberto goes to this place? (2)
9. What does his mother think about the situation. (2)
10. What does Roberto think? (1)

Read the following carefully. DO NOT translate but answer the questions in ENGLISH.

> *Rodrigo Amor y Sara M. de Amor se complacen en invitarle a usted y a su distinguida familia a la celebración del quinceañero*
>
> *de su hija*
>
> **MARÍA DE LOS ÁNGELES**
>
> *La recepción tendrá lugar el 16 de enero de 1998 de 6 p.m. a 8 p.m.; el baile de 8 p.m. a 12 medianoche en los salones del Club Campestre Los Pinos, 84 Vía de las Rosas, Pedregal de San Marcos.*

1. What is being announced? (1)
2. Who is making the announcement? (1)
3. Who are they? (1)
4. Why is the announcement being made? (1)
5. Who is María de los Ángeles? (2)
6. In which month will the event take place? (1)
7. What will happen between 6 - 8 p.m.? (2)
8. What will happen at 8 p.m.? (2)
9. Where will this take place? (2)
10. What is the location? (2)

Read the following carefully. DO NOT translate but answer the questions in ENGLISH.

PEDRITO'S SURPRISE

Una tarde, mientras Pedrito regresaba de la escuela, pensaba que un día iba a ser rico. Decidió compartir su dinero con su abuelita que lo cuidaba desde que murió su mama.

De repente vio a un hombre bajo que llevaba un sombrero grande. Pedrito, un poco miedoso, seguía caminando. Cuando estaba muy cerca del hombre, éste le dio un pequeño paquete.

Al llegar a su casa, Pedrito lo abrió y vio adentro un diamante enorme. El muchacho se dio cuenta de que el hombre era su padre que había salido hace muchos años a buscar su fortuna en el extranjero.

1. When did the story take place? (2)
2. Where was Pedrito coming from? (1)
3. What was Pedrito thinking? (1)
4. What decision did he make? (2)
5. With whom was Pedrito living? (1)
6. Describe the person Pedrito saw. (2)
7. What did Pedrito find inside the package? (1)
8. What did Pedrito realise? (2)
9. Where had Pedrito's father gone? (2)
10. Why had he gone there? (1)

Read the following carefully. DO NOT translate but answer the questions in ENGLISH.

El hotel más lujoso y espectacular de Isla de Perlas

¡Donde se hospedará la excelencia!

- Ubicado en la Avenida San Gabriel, a orillas de la Bahía Dorada, en plena área comercial, bancaria y financiera, cerca de los centros nocturnos, teatros y demás sitios de interés turístico.
- 185 Suites y lujosas habitaciones.
- Restaurante Gourmet
- Pub
- Salones para eventos
- Exclusivo y elegante centro de negocios.
- Dos espectaculares piscinas.
- Cancha de tenis
- La más moderna Marina y Club de Yates para pesca y deportes acuáticos.

Apertura junio de 1996

1. In addition to a hotel, what else is Flores?		(1)
2. Where is the hotel located?		(2)
3. What is its relation to the Bahía Dorada?		(1)
4. Name two places near the hotel.		(2)
5. What is said about the rooms?		(1)
6. What eating facilities are available?		(2)
7. When did the hotel start operating?		(1)
8. What are two of the sporting events offered by the hotel?		(2)
9. Is the hotel in the city or the country?		(1)
10. Why are yachts provided?		(2)

Read the following carefully. DO NOT translate but answer the questions in ENGLISH.

FIRE NEXT DOOR!

Una noche los miembros de la familia Roca fueron despertados por gritos que venían de la casa de los vecinos. Los niños abrieron la ventana de su habitación y vieron a los vecinos quienes estaban acercándose a su casa. El señor Amor gritaba
- ¡Socorro! ¡Fuego!

El Señor Amor tenía sus dos hijos en los brazos. El niño estaba llorando y gritando:
- ¡Papí los juguetes, quiero mis juguetes!, ¡Quiero mis juguetes!
La niña gritaba:
- ¿Dónde está mamá? ¿Dónde está mamá?
El señor Roca abrió la puerta y les dijo:
- Entren, entren. ¡Dios mío! Siéntense. Voy a llamar a los bomberos.
Raúl le dijo: - Papá ya lo hice, y casi inmediatamente se oyó la sirena del coche de bomberos.

1. What awoke the Roca family? (2)
2. What did the children do? (1)
3. What did they see? (1)
4. What was Mr. Amor shouting? (1)
5. Why was the boy crying? (1)
6. Who opened the door? (1)
7. What did this person do next? (2)
8. What did he intend to do? (2)
9. What did Raul tell him? (2)
10. What was heard? (2)

Read the following carefully. DO NOT translate but answer the questions in ENGLISH.

El señor Roberto Mena y la señora Ana Mena
le invitan a usted y a su apreciada familia
al enlace matrimonial de su hija

CARMEN

con el señor

CARLOS MORALES LÓPEZ

hijo del señor Eduardo López y la señora
Lisa Morales de López

La ceremonia se efectuará el sábado 26 de noviembre de
1998 a las cinco de la tarde en la Iglesia del Sagrado Corazón.
Se ruega pasar luego a una recepción en casa de
los padres de la novia, 234 Avenida Los Robles, Alajuela.

---

1. What is being sent? (1)
2. What is the occasion? (1)
3. When will it take place? (2)
4. Where will it take place? (1)
5. What event follows? (1)
6. Where will it take place? (2)
7. Where is this place located? (2)
8. Who is Carmen? (1)
9. Who is Carlos Morales López? (2)
10. Who are Eduardo López and Lisa Morales de López? (2)

Read the following carefully. DO NOT translate but answer the questions in ENGLISH.

Casa de Oro
Avenida Central
Número 2
Colombia

Querido Zacarías,

Deseo darle un cordial y amistoso saludo. Estoy muy contenta aquí en Colombia. Mi nueva amiga Carla es muy simpática y su familia es muy agradable. Su casa es muy bonita y tienen muchas fotos de diferentes partes del Caribe. He pasado dos semanas en Bogotá pero mañana vamos a Cali. La abuela de Carla vive allí y vamos a pasar una semana con ella.

Saludos a tu familia y escríbeme pronto.

Tu amiga,

María

---

1. Where is María? (2)
2. How does she feel about being at this place? (1)
3. Who are the persons that she has met? (2)
4. How does she describe them? (2)
5. What do these persons have in their house? (2)
6. How long has María been at this place? (1)
7. Where will she go next? (1)
8. Who lives there? (1)
9. How long will María spend at this place? (1)
10. What does María want Zacarías to do? (2)

Read the following carefully. DO NOT translate but answer the questions in ENGLISH.

**SANTA CLARA
LA ISLA HECHA
PARA SER AMADA**

UNA PORCIÓN DE TIERRA DULCE RODEADA DE SONRISA POR TODAS PARTES.

ESTA ISLA TIENE 30 KILÓMETROS DE LARGO POR UNA SONRISA DE ANCHO.

SANTA CLARA LE BRINDA TODO: SU SUAVE CLIMA...
SU AIRE LIMPIO Y RENOVADOR...
SUS HERMOSAS PLAYAS ACOGEDORAS... EL SOL BENIGNO, SIEMPRE PRESENTE

TIENDAS A PRECIO DE PUERTO LIBRE.

VENGA A SANTA CLARA - LA ISLA DE GENTE CORDIAL. PARA TODA LA FAMILIA.

LOS ANTIGÜENSES NO NECESITAN VISA.
HAY 5 VUELOS SEMANALES.
(TWIA Y CARA).
VEA A SU AGENTE DE VIAJES.

SANTA CLARA
LA BELLA
DONDE LA FELICIDAD SE QUEDÓ A VIVIR.
DIRECCIÓN DE TURISMO DE SANTA CLARA, PARQUE CENTRAL
EDIFICIO HILTON (EMBAJADA DE SANTA CLARA)
PENT HOUSE - TEL. 327.04.96

1. What is given as the size of Santa Clara in the advertisement? (1)
2. What are prices in shops like and why is this so? (2)
3. What suggests that visitors will be happy? (2)
4. What is said about the weather in Santa Clara? (1)
5. What is the air like in Santa Clara? (1)
6. In addition to being beautiful, what else is said about the beaches? (2)
7. To what age groups is the advertisement directed? (2)
8. How often can Antiguans go to Santa Clara? (1)
9. Why is it easy for them to go? (1)
10. Where can interested persons get more information? (2)

Read the following carefully. DO NOT translate but answer the questions in ENGLISH.

A CUALQUIER PAÍS DEL MUNDO

LA GRAN AEROLÍNEA PALACIO

¡A TODOS LOS PAÍSES DEL MUNDO!

- Sólo Palacio le ofrece un servicio exclusivo
- Exquisitas comidas
- Finos vinos
- Cine en inglés y en español
- Música estereofónica tanto en la clase turística como en la primera clase

Palacio también le ofrece un programa para ganar viajes gratis a América Latina y otros destinos internacionales.

Vuela con Palacio siempre.
Es seguro.
No olvidará el vuelo nunca.
Llámanos ahora a nuestra oficina: 555-212-345

PALACIO

Las alas del Mundo

1. What is being advertised? (1)
2. What is its name? (1)
3. Name two things which are offered. (2)
4. What is offered in two languages? (1)
5. What entertainment is available? (2)
6. What is offered in both classes? (1)
7. What special programme is also being offered? (2)
8. Why should people use this service? (2)
9. What will people never forget? (1)
10. What are people asked to do immediately? (2)

Read the following carefully. DO NOT translate but answer the questions in ENGLISH.

VENDA MA$
MOTIVE Y ORGANICE A SUS VENDEDORES

SEMINARIO

"VENTAS MI PROFESIÓN"
¡Con 15 años de experiencia capacitando Vendedores!

Temas
* Factores para triunfar en Ventas.
* Planes de acción y objetivos.
* Organización del tiempo y reportes

LUGAR: Hotel del Bosque - Melchor Ocampo 323, México, DF 03100

DÍA: 23 de febrero de 8:30 A.M. a 6:30 P.M.

COSTO: N$ 600 + I.V.A

INSCRIPCIONES: Avenida Pesado No. 110-1c Col. Del Valle, México, D.F. 03100

Tel./Fax 523-7632 687-1550 682-9851 669-1828

1. To whom is the advertisement directed? (1)
2. What is this person encouraged to do? (2)
3. What is being advertised? (2)
4. Where will the event take place? (2)
5. What does the person advertising say about himself? (2)
6. What are two topics which will be dealt with during the event? (2)
7. What is the cost of attending the event? (1)
8. What can be achieved by attending? (1)
9. How can the advertiser be contacted? (1)
10. How long will the event last? (1)

Read the following carefully. DO NOT translate but answer the questions in ENGLISH.

AVENTURAS DE NAVEGACIÓN

Puede descubrir las maravillas de la navegación en estilo y comodidad a bordo de uno de nuestros barcos de lujo.

**CRUCERO DE MAGNOLIS
LE OFRECE**

CRUCEROS MÁGICOS A DOSCIENTOS DESTINOS DIFERENTES.

Ofrecemos durante todo el año:

- Precios bajos
- Personales agradables
- Una experiencia inolvidable.

Esperamos su llamada a nuestra oficina.   888-559-222
O si prefiere, visítenos. Estamos a la orden.

Calle Quinto, Número 8.

1. What does this advertisement offer? (1)
2. How will passengers travel? (1)
3. How are the ships described? (1)
4. What is the name of the company which placed this advertisement? (2)
5. What is being advertised? (1)
6. How many different places are mentioned in the offer? (1)
7. Name two things the company offers. (2)
8. When is the offer available? (1)
9. Where is the company located? (2)
10. How can one obtain further information? (2)

Read the following carefully. DO NOT translate but answer the questions in ENGLISH.

La vida en la región donde vivía el Hermano Anansi era muy difícil. No llovía y las plantas, la tierra y toda la vegetación estaban secas. No había nada como alimento para los animales que sufrían de hambre. Un día el Hermano Anansi y el Hermano Perro se dieron cuenta de que había un maizal al otro lado del río. El Hermano Perro se ofreció a llevar a Anansi en la espalda al otro lado del río. Al llegar al maizal Anansi y el Hermano Perro seleccionaron los mejores mazorcas de maíz. Pero Anansi no quería compartir el maíz con el Hermano Perro. Cuando el Hermano Perro empezó a comer el maíz, el Hermano Anansi empezó a gritar para llamar la atención del dueño del maizal.

Cuando el amo oyó los gritos de Anansi corrió al maizal con un palo grueso que usó para golpear al Hermano Perro mientras el Hermano Anansi se escondió. Cuando el dueño salió con el pobre Hermano Perro como prisionero, Anansi se quedó en la granja y todos los días comía el maíz con alegría.

1. Describe the area in which Anansi lived. (2)
2. Why was it like this? (2)
3. What problem did this situation create? (2)
4. What did Anansi discover? (2)
5. Who discovered this with him? (1)
6. How did Hermano Anansi get across the river? (1)
7. What did they do when they got there? (1)
8. What did Anansi do afterwards? (1)
9. Why did he do this? (1)
10. What happened to Hermano Perro? (2)

Read the following carefully. DO NOT translate but answer the questions in ENGLISH.

GRAN JEFE

SU VIAJE A PAULINA EN PRIMERA CLASE

De Puerto Verde a San Pedro en sólo dos horas. Sin colas y sin pérdidas de tiempo. Disfrute del más lujoso y confortable viaje en la exclusiva flota Gran Jefe, que ahora cuenta con tres unidades.

Gran Jefe, un estupendo viaje en auténtica primera clase, con televisión a color y la fabulosa atención de nuestras atractivas y simpáticas nautimozas.

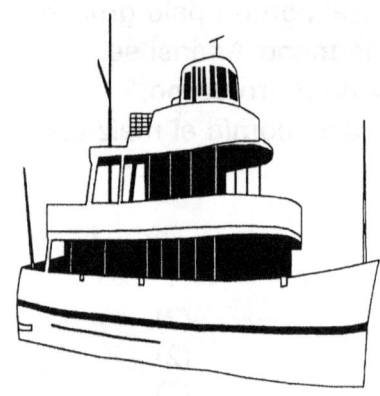

TURISMO SAN PEDRO C.A. LA EMPRESA GRANDE DE ORIENTE

Puerto Verde
Hotel Melía, Local 3 Principal
Teléfono: (081) 24.241
Terminal MOCARA
Final Av. Principal del Paraíso

Punta de Salima
Terminal Muelle
Teléfono: (095) 98.128

San Juan
Calle Marcano, a una cuadra de la Plaza Central
Teléfono: (095) 23.461

1. Where does the trip start? (1)
2. How long is the trip? (1)
3. Where is the company which placed the advertisment located? (1)
4. What will the traveller be saved? (2)
5. What is authentic about this trip? (2)
6. Who attends to passengers? (1)
7. What is said about them? (2)
8. What is provided to entertain passengers? (2)
9. Where is the port located in San Juan? (2)
10. How many boats does the company have? (1)

Read the following carefully. DO NOT translate but answer the questions in ENGLISH.

NUEVA OFICINA DEL BANCO OPINIÓN
2000 AVENIDA CENTRAL

OFRECE TODOS LOS SERVICIOS BANCARIOS
A LOS CLIENTES DEL BANCO OPINIÓN
Las puertas se abrirán el 10 de agosto de 1998

- Cuentas corrientes
- Cuentas de ahorro
- Transferencias
- Certificados de Depósitos y mucho más.
- Impuestos bajos

Para Información Adicional, Favor llamar: 552 7711

BANCO OPINIÓN - EL BANCO DE CONFIANZA

1. What is being advertised? (2)
2. What is the name of the company which placed this advertisement? (1)
3. When will these services become available? (2)
4. What are low in this company? (2)
5. What kind of services does this company provide? (2)
6. Name two of these services. (2)
7. Where is this company located? (1)
8. Why is the number 552 7711 included? (1)
9. How is the company described? (1)
10. How do we know that the company offers other services besides the ones specified? (1)

Read the following carefully. DO NOT translate but answer the questions in ENGLISH.

Altaña Tennis Club

La Junta Directiva y Socios del Altaña Tennis Club, cumplen con el penoso deber de participar el sensible fallecimiento de la señora

Paloma Salazar
(Q.E.P.D)

Madre de nuestro consocio Ricardo Salazar, a quien hacemos llegar nuestras más sentidas expresiones de condolencia, extensiva a su esposa e hijos, demás familiares y amigos.

Caracas, 9 de diciembre de 1997.

1. Who placed this announcement? (2)
2. What are they expressing? (1)
3. What is their connection with Ricardo Salazar? (2)
4. Who is Paloma Salazar? (1)
5. What has happened to her? (1)
6. What obligation are the two groups fulfilling? (2)
7. Why is this obligation considered 'penoso'? (1)
8. What is the meaning of Q.E.P.D.? (2)
9. Who are the main persons to whom the announcement is directed? (2)
10. Who else is referred to? (1)

Read the following carefully. DO NOT translate but answer the questions in ENGLISH.

**Hasta
un hombre
invisible
necesita
estar
cubierto**

¡Cúbrase por
completo!

A pesar de sus extraños poderes,
un hombre invisible sabe que él también
puede sufrir un accidente:
su transparencia no es más que una
forma de protección.
Así como un hombre invisible trata de estar
cubierto, asimismo usted y su familia
necesitan sentirse seguros.
Un seguro de Vida y una póliza Contra Accidentes
son la mejor manera de demostrar todo
el amor que usted siente por los suyos. Consulte con su
Productor y él le dirá por qué
SEGUROS ÁGUILA es cobertura segura.
Hasta los superhéroes necesitan estar cubiertos...
cúbrase usted también con SEGUROS ÁGUILA.
**Siéntase Superseguro Y Cúbrase Por
Completo Con**

SEGUROS ÁGUILA

1. What is the name of the company that has placed this advertisement? (1)
2. What is the business of this company? (1)
3. What is the invisible man said to have? (2)
4. What could happen to the invisible man? (1)
5. Why is being invisible not enough? (2)
6. What are the two types of protection the company is offering? (2)
7. What is a good way of showing love for your family? (2)
8. What is said about superheroes? (1)
9. To whom is the advertisement directed? (1)
10. How will you feel if you take the advice in the advertisement? (2)

Read the following carefully. DO NOT translate but answer the questions in ENGLISH.

PREPARING TO MAKE "AREBA"

Una actividad importante en la vida de los garífunas es la preparación del pan de yuca. Este pan seco llamado "areba" se prepara con la raíz de la yuca, una planta que se cultiva en los trópicos como alimento y es un legado de los indios caribes.

La preparación del pan es un largo proceso que comienza con la cosecha de las raíces de la yuca. Por lo general, las mujeres y los niños se levantan antes del amanecer y se dirigen a las granjas que en Belice están situadas en medio de la selva, entre ocho y quince kilómetros de los pueblos. A la sombra de las palmas, recogen de dieciocho a veinte kilógramos de raíces de yuca. Cuando terminan, llevan la yuca en canastas sobre la cabeza hasta la aldea.

Al llegar a las aldeas, para protegerse del sol van debajo de las casas que son construídas sobre postes. Allí las mujeres y los niños pelan y lavan las raíces. Después las rallan sobre planchas de madera con piedras agudas. Las mujeres acompañan el trabajo con canciones en que hablan de la tristeza y de la vida en general.

1. What is "Areba" (1)
2. What do the garífunas use to prepare it? (1)
3. Where is this grown and for what purpose? (2)
4. How does the process of preparing "areba" begin? (1)
5. Who are involved in this process? (2)
6. Approximately how much of the crop is reaped? (2)
7. Where are the farms usually located in Belize? (2)
8. Why do the women and children go under the house? (1)
9. What two things do they do there first? (2)
10. What do the women do as they work? (1)

Read the following carefully. DO NOT translate but answer the questions in ENGLISH.

41742

ESTADO DE CUENTA

Hotel CONTINENTAL
☆☆☆☆☆☆
Guayaquil - Ecuador

Chile y 10 de Agosto Esquina Tel: 329270
Casilla-09-01-4510 Telefax: 04-325454

HABIT No.	NOMBRE	PERS./TARIFA
712	Felipe González Amor	1/488000
RECEPCIONISTA	SALIDA 29 de nov. de 1998	LLEGADA 21 de nov. de 1998
OBSERVACIONES		

	FECHA	CONCEPTO	CARGOS	ABONOS	SALDO	SALDO ANTERIOR
1	NOV.22.98	COMU 712	*2,800.00		*2,889.00	***2,880.00
2	NOV.22.98	HABIT 712	488,000.00			
3	NOV.22.98	SERVC 712	*48,800.00			
4	NOV.22.98	IMPTO 712	*48,800.00		588,480.00*	*588,480.00
5	NOV.23.98	COMU 712	28,800.00		617,280.00	*617,280.00
6	NOV.23.98	CAJA 712		617,280.00	* .00	
7	NOV.25.98	LAVAN	30,000.00			
8	NOV.26.98	CAFETERIA	22,000.00			
9						
10						
11						
12						

SÍMBOLOS: REG. UNIC. No. 0990000085001

HABIT:	HABITACIÓN	R.SERV:	SERVICIO HABITAC	FIRMA DEL HUESPED
PENS:	PENSIÓN	COMUN:	COMUNICACIONES	F. González
SERV:	SERVICIO	LAVAN:	LAVANDERÍA	
IMPTO:	IMPUESTO	VARS:	VARIOS	
CAFET:	CAFETERÍA	DESE:	DESEMBOLSOS	DIRECCIÓN: Apartado 10. Calle Madrid
C-BAR:	COMEDOR BAR	PROP:	PROPINAS	
DESC:	DESCUENTO			APROBADO POR: Raúl López Mena

1. What is being shown? (2 marks)
2. Which place has prepared this document and for whom? (2 marks)
3. What is the address of this place? (2 marks)
4. When did this person arrive there? (2 marks)
5. Where did he/she occupy? (1 mark)
6. How much was charged for tax? (2 marks)
7. Why was 2,800.00 sucres recorded on November 22? (1 mark)
8. How much was spent in the cafeteria on November 26? (1 mark)
9. On what was 30,000 sucres spent on November 25? (1 mark)
10. What was the cost of the place where the person stayed? (1 mark)

Read the following carefully. DO NOT translate but answer the questions in ENGLISH.

```
BANCO DEL PACÍFICO                    98/11/23
                                      Fecha
                                      No. 1117090
         COMPROBANTE DE NEGOCIACIÓN DE DIVISAS

Nombre del Cliente: _____ Michael Ramsay _____

C.I/R.U.C./Pasaporte No. _____ 211100432 _____

Dirección __ 7 Carnation Path, Kingston 7, Jamaica __ Teléfono __ 809-92-77777 __
```

TIPO DE TRANSACCIÓN

Compra ☐   Venta ✓
Billete ☐   Cheque ☐   Otros ☐

Moneda	Valor en Moneda Extranjera	Tipo de Cambio	Valor en Moneda Nacional
	US$40	6273	250.QW

INSTRUCCIONES DEL CLIENTE

☐ Débito a Cuenta: ☐ Crédito a Cuenta:

  Tipo ____ No. _____   Tipo ____ No. __ 412018-9 Sucres __

  Tipo ____ No. _____   Tipo ____ No. _____

☐ Efectivo _____   ☐ Cheque _____

Observaciones _____

Tipo: A=Ahorros   C=Corriente   D=Dólares

Autorizo a efectuar la transacción en Divisas de acuerdo a instruciones.

Declaro que los fondos de esta operación bancaria tienen origen o destino lícito.

                                                    M. Ramsay
_____   _____
 Elaborado por   Firma del Cliente

1. What is being shown? (2 marks)
2. Who did the transaction? (1 mark)
3. What does the number 211100432 represent? (2 marks)
4. In which country does the person reside? (1 mark)
5. What kind of transaction did he do? (2 marks)
6. What does 6273 represent? (2 marks)
7. What did the person receive? (2 marks)
8. What does the person declare when he signs? (3 marks)

Read the following carefully. DO NOT translate but answer the questions in ENGLISH.

ZONA

REPÚBLICA DE PANAMÁ
DEPARTMENTO DE MIGRACIÓN
TARJETA INTERNACIONAL DE EMBARQUE/DESEMBARQUE

Título
Sr. ☐   Srta. ✓
Sra. ☐   Otro ☐

FAVOR USAR LETRA DE MOLDE   Sexo   M ☐   F ✓

NOMBRE COMPLETO: **RAMÍREZ LÓPEZ**
Apellidos

ÁNGELA MARÍA
Nombres

PAÍS DE NACIMIENTO: _Costa Rica_   Edad _22_
NACIONALIDAD: _Costarricense_   OCUPACIÓN: _Periodista_
NÚMERO DE FAMILIARES QUE VIAJA CON Vd. _____
DOMICILIO PERMANENTE: _San José_   _Heredia_   _Costa Rica_
Ciudad   Prov. O Estado   País
DIRECCIÓN POSTAL: _Apartado 1346, Escazú, San José_
PASAPORTE No. _2234560_   LUGAR DE EXPEDICIÓN: _San José - Costa Rica_
MOTIVO DE VIAJE   RECREO ☐   NEGOCIOS ☐
CONVENCIONES ✓   OTROS _Posibilidad de Obtener Empleo_
Especifique
TIEMPO DE ESTADÍA EN PANAMÁ: _Siete_ DÍAS
PUERTO DE EMBARQUE: _San José, Costa Rica_
DOMICILIO EN PANAMA: _Hotel Solar_

INFORMACIÓN DE SALIDA (Adicional)

PAÍS Y CIUDAD DE DESTINO: _____
TIEMPO DE ESTADÍA EN ESE LUGAR: _____
COMPAÑÍA _____ VUELO No. _____
PAZ Y SALVO No. _____

---

1. What type of form is being shown? (2 marks)
2. Which agency issued this form? (2 marks)
3. What is the full name of the person who is completing the form? (2 marks)
4. In which country was the person born? (1 mark)
5. What is the person's profession? (1 mark)
6. How many other family members are travelling with the person? (1 mark)
7. Where does the person live in his/her country? (2 marks)
8. State two reasons why the person is travelling to Panama. (2 marks)
9. How long will the person be in Panama? (1 mark)
10. Where does the person intend to stay in Panama? (1 mark)

Read the following carefully. DO NOT translate but answer the questions in ENGLISH.

Cuéntanos tu historia
de amor
y viaja gratis
a
Sudamérica

Casa de Lujo, uno de los complejos turísticos más lujosos del Ecuador, te recibirá durante una semana, si nos cuentas tu mejor historia de amor.

Seguro que tienes alguna anécdota romántica o divertida del momento en que miraste por primera vez a tu novio o novia. Queremos que todos nuestros lectores que están planificando la boda nos escriban. El punto de vista masculino nos interesa muchísimo.

Entre todas las cartas recibidas, con las mejores historias de amor se sorteará un viaje PARA DOS PERSONAS A CASA DE LUJO. ¡Participa y haz un viaje de sueño a Sudamérica. Esperamos tus cartas hasta el 20 de junio.

Casa de Lujo
P.O. Box 149
Quito, Ecuador

1. What is this advertisement inviting readers to do? (2 marks)
2. Which company has placed this advertisement? (1 mark)
3. Which readers is this advertisement targeting? (2 marks)
4. What kind of company is it? (2 marks)
5. What kinds of stories do they want their readers to share? (2 marks)
6. What is of particular interest to them? (2 marks)
7. What will the writer/writers of the best story receive? (2 marks)
8. What will happen on June 20? (2 marks)

Read the following carefully. DO NOT translate but answer the questions in ENGLISH.

PUEDE SER TUYO

¡UN TRAJE DE BODA FABULOSO!

Dimitrio Gambril es el diseñador de trajes de novia preferido por la alta sociedad. Las novias elegantes y sofisticadas se casan en sus vestidos espectaculares. Tienen ricos bordados y cortes precisos que acentúan la ligereza del talle. Hay diseños modernos con damascos y brocados; hay diseños suntuosos para dar el sí el día más feliz de tu vida. Uno de estos vestidos espléndidos puede ser tuyo, hecho a medida, a un precio bajo. Es un regalo para la novia elegante que no tiene mucho dinero. Una oferta increíble.

¡Llámenos a nuestro salón!

Dimitrio Gambril
Avenida Sur
28006 Santiago, Chile
43505 00.

1. What is being advertised? (2 marks)
2. Who is Dimitrio Gambril? (2 marks)
3. What is special about this product? (2 marks)
4. What two types of materials are named? (2 marks)
5. How are these products made? (2 marks)
6. Who is being offered this product at a low price? (2 marks)
7. What should interested persons do? (2 marks)
8. In which part of the country is the designer located? (1 mark)

READING COMPREHENSION

GENERAL PROFICIENCY

Candidates are required to answer questions based on a continuous passage.

Questions will be in Spanish and answers are to be written in Spanish.
This section corresponds to **Paper 2, Section 3 and is worth 15 marks.**

Read the passage carefully and then answer the questions in Spanish **using your own words.**

- ¡Eres muy malo! ¡Eres muy necio! gritó el papá de Pepito. Pepito había roto un florero de cristal que pertenecía a la abuela de su papá. Su papá estaba muy enojado porque Pepito siempre rompía algún objeto de gran valor en la casa.

Pepito decidió que iba a huir de casa. No le gustaba que su padre le gritara. Se sentía muy mal porque había roto algo con tanto valor.

Durante la noche cuando todos estaban dormidos Pepito se levantó y buscó la maleta. Arregló toda la ropa favorita que quería llevar con él. Atravesaba el suelo de puntillas cuando oyó una voz que le decía:
- Si sales de la casa no puedes volver.

Pepito se detuvo. Cuando dio una vuelta completa no vio a nadie pero sabía que era la voz de su papá.

- Te queremos mucho, pero a veces nos pones furiosos. Es verdad que te gritamos cuando estamos enojados pero esto no quiere decir que no te queramos. Debes tratar de tener más cuidado.

Pepito se quedó pensando. En realidad él no quería huir de la casa. A él le gustaba su casa. Entonces, decidió y dijo.
- No, no voy a salir. Voy a quedarme aquí y voy a tratar de tener cuidado y de ser más agradable.

Preguntas

1. ¿Por qué el papá de Pepito le gritó? (1)
2. ¿A quién pertenecía el florero? (2)
3. ¿Qué pensaba hacer Pepito? (2)
4. ¿Cuándo se levantó Pepito y por qué? (2)
5. ¿Qué decidió poner en la maleta? (2)
6. ¿Quién le habló cuando iba a salir? (2)
7. ¿Qué le gustaba a Pepito? (2)
8. ¿Cuál fue la decisión de Pepito? (2)

Read the passage carefully and then answer the questions in Spanish **using your own words.**

Ayer, por la mañana, dos hombres vestidos de gris, entraron en una joyería situada en el centro de la ciudad, cerca de la Avenida Tijuana.

Según un testigo que estaba en la joyería durante el atraco, uno de los hombres se acercó al gerente de la joyería y le ordenó que le diera todas las joyas que estaban en la vitrina. Además, los clientes tenían que quitarse sus propias joyas y ponerlas en un saco que el otro ladrón llevaba. Lo raro era que el guardia que trabajaba para la empresa, sacó un revólver y disparó dos veces. Una de las balas hirió al gerente en la rodilla.

Los tres salieron con una cantidad de joyas incluso relojes suizos de primera calidad, pendientes y anillos de oro. Escaparon en un auto que les esperaba afuera con el motor arrancado. La policía sigue buscando a los ladrones y pide al público que le dé cualquier información que tenga. También hay una recompensa para quien tenga información acerca del asunto.

Preguntas

1. ¿Cuándo ocurrió el robo? (1)
2. ¿Qué mandó hacer el ladrón al gerente? (2)
3. ¿Qué tuvieron que hacer los clientes? (2)
4. ¿Por qué parecía rara, la acción de la persona con el revólver? (2)
5. ¿Qué le pasó al gerente de la joyería? (2)
6. ¿Qué clase de joyas tomaron los ladrones? (2)
7. ¿Cómo escaparon los ladrones? (2)
8. ¿Qué pide la policía? (2)

Read the passage carefully and then answer the questions in Spanish **using your own words**.

Querida Lourdes,

Aquí estamos en México y lo estamos pasando bien. El domingo pasado fuimos a Izamal en tren y fue un viaje maravilloso.

Llegamos a la estación de Mérida a las siete de la mañana y el tren arrancó media hora después de nuestra llegada.

El viaje duró dos horas y al llegar a nuestro destino, había una banda de músicos para entretenernos. Además, el director de turismo de Izamal estaba en la estación para darnos la bienvenida.

Recorrimos todo el pueblo en calesas que son bonitos carros de muchos colores tirados por caballos. Vimos la iglesia más vieja de la Provincia, unos edificios antiguos y la artesanía de los indios. Te compré un regalo. Almorzamos a la una y la comida estaba muy sabrosa. Yo comí pollo con salsa verde y de postre, helado de vainilla y pastel.

Así que, Lourdes, este intercambio de estudiantes me ha ayudado muchísimo. Ojalá tú estes aprendiendo mucho inglés en Jamaica y divirtiéndote tanto como yo.

Escríbeme pronto y saluda a todos de mi parte.

Recibe un abrazo cariñoso de tu amiga,

Kelly-Ann

Preguntas

1. ¿Cómo llegaron los visitantes a Izamal? (1)
2. ¿A qué hora salió? (2)
3. ¿A qué hora llegaron a Izamal? (2)
4. ¿Quiénes estaban en la estación para saludar a los viajeros? (2)
5. Describe las calesas. (2)
6. Después de comer pollo, ¿qué más comió Kelly-Ann? (2)
7. ¿Cómo estaba el almuerzo? (2)
8. ¿Qué hace Lourdes en Jamaica? (2)

Read the passage carefully and then answer the questions in Spanish **using your own words.**

Una tarde después de un almuerzo grande de mosquitos y moscas Moho, el sapo, se escondió al lado de la charca para dormir la siesta. Estaba soñando con la cena cuando de repente se despertó asustado. Sentía algo en la espalda. ¿Será una hoja? se preguntó. De pronto oyó un sonido que reconoció como la voz del niño que siempre jugaba en la charca. Muy lentamente abrió los ojos y vio la cara de un ser humano. ¡Qué horror! Se dio cuenta de que el niño lo había atrapado.

Moho se dijo - ¡Qué niño atrevido! Me despertó de la siesta para que jugara con él. Es obvio que está cansado de los peces y quiere molestarme. Se acordó de la última vez que una niña lo había capturado. Ella lo llevó a su casa donde pasó dos días. Fueron los peores días de su vida. La niña no le permitió buscar las moscas para la comida y casi se murió de hambre. Cuando logró escaparse juró que nunca volvería a la casa de otro ser humano y ahora le iba a pasar el mismo horror....

Preguntas

1. ¿Por qué se escondió el sapo después del almuerzo? (1)
2. ¿Qué hacía el sapo antes de que fuera despertado? (2)
3. ¿Cómo se despertó? (2)
4. ¿Por qué pensaba que había una hoja en la espalda? (2)
5. ¿Quién hacía sonidos? (2)
6. ¿Qué le gustaba hacer a esta persona? (2)
7. ¿Quién había capturado al sapo antes? (2)
8. ¿Cuándo pasó el sapo los peores días de su vida? (2)

Read the passage carefully and then answer the questions in Spanish **using your own words.**

El Hermano Anansi y el Hermano Pájaro eran grandes enemigos. El Hermano Pájaro siempre se quejaba del día cuando el Hermano Anansi le engañó y le dijo a todo el mundo que El Hermano Anansi nunca tendría la oportunidad de volver a hacerlo.

El Hermano Anansi dijo que estaba harto de las quejas del Hermano Pájaro y decidió que iba a mostrarle que era el Rey de las trampas y que podía burlarse de una persona muchas veces.

Mandó a decirle al Hermano Pájaro que su mamá había muerto y que necesitaba su ayuda con el funeral. El Hermano Pájaro era muy simpático y se decidió a ayudar a Anansi.

Mientras esperaba la llegada del Hermano Pájaro, Anansi se vistió de la ropa de su mamá y se tumbó en la cama.

Cuando el Hermano Pájaro llegó a la casa del Hermano Anansi una de sus hermanas le recibió y le mostró a la mamá en la cama.
    - Lo siento mucho - le dijo el Hermano Pájaro
En ese momento el Hermano Anansi se levantó y le dijo tranquilamente:
    - Deja de decirle a todo el mundo que yo soy malo.
El Hermano Pájaro se asustó y gritó con temor. Cuando se dio cuenta de que el Hermano Anansi le había engañado otra vez, juró que nunca volvería a hablar ni con él, ni con los otros miembros de su familia.

Preguntas

1. ¿Cómo era la relación entre el Hermano Anansi y el Hermano Pájaro? (1)
2. ¿Qué pensaba el Hermano Pájaro que Anansi no podía hacerle otra vez? (2)
3. ¿Qué decidió hacer el Hermano Anansi? (2)
4. ¿Cómo era el Hermano Pájaro? (2)
5. ¿Cómo reaccionó el Hermano Pájaro cuando pensaba que la mamá del Hermano Anansi estaba muerto? (2)
6. ¿Quién estaba en la cama? (2)
7. ¿Por qué se asustó el Hermano Pájaro? (2)
8. ¿Qué decidío el Hermano Pájaro? (2)

Read the passage carefully and then answer the questions in Spanish **using your own words.**

La familia de Carmen vivía en un pueblo pequeño y bello. Allí había todas las comodidades de la vida moderna. A los padres les encantaba su casa. La compraron a una anciana cuyos bisabuelos la construyeron durante el siglo 19. Los visitantes al pueblo siempre se detenían enfrente de la casa para sacar fotos y siempre comentaban la belleza de la casa. Pero Carmen y su familia tenían un problema serio - los vecinos ruidosos.

Los vecinos se levantaban cada día gritando y peleando. Además armaban mucho bullicio mientras se peleaban entre ellos. La familia de Carmen pensaba mudarse pero no querían dejar su casa preciosa.

Un día, se le ocurrió una idea al papá y la compartió con la familia. Iba a pasar una semana grabando todo el ruido que venía de la casa de los vecinos. Después tocaría la grabación para que los vecinos la escucharan.

Cuando los vecinos escucharon la grabación, se sintieron muy avergonzados y desde ese día cesaron de hacer tanto ruido. La vecindad volvió a estar tranquila y la familia de Carmen decidió quedarse en su casa encantadora.

Preguntas

1. ¿Cómo era el pueblo? (1)
2. ¿Qué les gustaba a los padres de Carmen? (2)
3. ¿Quiénes construyeron la casa en donde vivía la familia? (2)
4. ¿Qué hacían los turistas? (2)
5. ¿Por qué pensaba la familia mudarse de la casa? (2)
6. ¿Qué decidió hacer el papá? (2)
7. ¿Qué efecto tenía la grabación en los vecinos? (2)
8. ¿Por qué decidió quedarse la familia de Carmen? (2)

Read the passage carefully and then answer the questions in Spanish **using your own words**.

Un día el Hermano Tacumá decidió cultivar un huerto delante de su casa. Decidió hacerlo porque a veces la situación del país se ponía muy dura y la gente padecía de hambre. El Hermano Tacumá quería tener una gran abundancia de comida para venderla y para dársela a los pobres.

El huerto era muy hermoso. Había mucho maíz, frijoles y zanahorias.
El Hermano Anansi visitaba al Hermano Tacumá con mucha frecuencia y siempre admiraba el huerto. Él no quería sembrar su propio huerto proque a él no le gustaba trabajar. Nunca había trabajado en la vida. Él deseaba comer las verduras que había en el huerto del Hermano Tacumá. Sin embargo, sabía que el Hermano Tacumá no les daría la comida a las personas perezosas como él. Entonces decidió volver al huerto durante la noche para recoger los productos del huerto del Hermano Tacumá.

Un día, el Hermano Tacumá se dio cuenta de que alguien le robaba las verduras por la noche. Decidió consultar al Hermano Anansi, quien era famoso en toda la región por su inteligencia.

El Hermano Anansi expresó sorpresa cuando escuchó el problema del Hermano Tacumá. Dijo que los ladrones eran sus peores enemigos. El Hermano Tacumá estaba contento cuando escuchó el consejo del Hermano Anansi. Pensó que fue una buena idea contratar a un guardia para cuidar el huerto durante la noche - como le recomendó el Hermano Anansi. Estaba muy contento cuando el Hermano Anansi se ofreció para hacer el trabajo.

Preguntas

1. ¿Dónde cultivó el Hermano Tacumá el huerto? (1)
2. ¿Qué pensaba hacer el Hermano Tacumá con las verduras? (2)
3. ¿Qué hacía el Hermano Anansi cuando le visitaba el Hermano Tacumá? (2)
4. ¿Qué no quería hacer el Hermano Anansi? (2)
5. ¿Qué descubrió el Hermano Tacumá? (2)
6. ¿Por qué consultó el Hermano Tacumá con el Hermano Anansi? (2)
7. ¿Qué consejo le dio el Hermano Anansi al Hermano Tacumá? (2)
8. ¿Por qué estaba contento el Hermano Tacumá? (2)

Read the passage carefully and then answer the questions in Spanish **using your own words.**

El verano pasado Raúl pasó las vacaciones con los abuelos en el campo. Todos los días se levantaba muy temprano para pasearse por la finca grande de los abuelos. Pasaba todas las mañanas mirando los pájaros, trepando los árboles y jugando con los barcos de papel en la pequeña charca que estaba en la granja. Se divertía de esta manera hasta que la abuela lo llamaba para desayunar.

Le gustaba mucho la comida que la abuela preparaba. Siempre le decía a ella que era la mejor cocinera del mundo. Toda la comida era deliciosa especialmente el pollo frito.

Todos los días después del desayuno, Raúl saliá con el abuelo, para atender los animales. Primero, el abuelo les daba de comer a los cerdos. Había más de veinte cerdos gordos y a Raúl le fascinaba ver las colitas que tenían forma de "s". Después iban a dar el maíz a las gallinas.

Un día el abuelo le dijo a Raúl que no se sentía bien y que quería que Raúl fuera a atender las gallinas. Raúl estaba contento porque quería demostrar al abuelo que era responsable. Salió corriendo de la casa.

Estaba a punto de abrir la puerta del gallinero cuando vio algo en el rincón. Se asustó cuando se dio cuenta de que era una culebra. No sabía qué hacer. No quería correr porque no quería atraer la culebra con los ruidos.

- ¿Qué voy a hacer? se preguntó. Se quedó ahí esperando y mirando los ojos espantosos de la culebra.
Después de un rato, oyó una risa que venía de afuera. Fue la voz de José, uno de los labradores quien le preguntó.
- ¿Qué pasa Raúl, tienes miedo de la goma?

Preguntas

1. ¿Qué hizo Raúl el verano pasado? (1)
2. ¿Qué hacía Raúl cada día? (2)
3. ¿Cómo pasaba las mañanas? (2)
4. ¿Qué opinión tenía de la abuela? (2)
5. ¿Qué quería el tío que Raúl hiciera un día? (2)
6. ¿Cómo reaccionó Raúl y por qué? (2)
7. ¿Qué vio Raúl en el gallinero? (2)
8. ¿Qué hacía mientras se quedaba esperando? (2)

Read the passage carefully and then answer the questions in Spanish **using your own words.**

Hacía tres semanas que el Hermano Anansi trabajaba en el huerto del Hermano Tacumá como guardía. Todos los días le decía al Hermano Tacumá que le gustaba su trabajo y que él era un buen jefe.

Pero había un problema - los robos continuaban. Un día el Hermano Anansi le dijo al Hermano Tacumá que él había visto al ladrón durante la noche pero no pudo detenerlo.

El Hermano Tacumá fue a consultar al Hermano Pájaro quien le dijo que en su opinión el Hermano Anansi era un gran bandido y que necesitaba emplear a un guardia para vigilar al Hermano Anansi. Él se ofreció para ayudar al Hermano Tacumá a montar una trampa para los ladrones.

En la noche el Hermano Pájaro fue al huerto y se escondió en un árbol. Cuando el Hermano Anansi llegó no vio al Hermano Pájaro. Anansi empezó a llenar un saco grande de maíz y el Hermano Pájaro voló a llamar al Hermano Tacumá. Cuando regresaron Anansi estaba listo para levantar el saco pesado cuando le gritaron:
     - ¡No te muevas ladrón!

Preguntas

1. ¿Cuánto tiempo hacía que el Hermano Tacumá trabajaba en la finca? (1)
2. ¿Qué le decía al Hermano Tacumá? (2)
3. ¿Qué le contó Anansi al Hermano Tacumá? (2)
4. ¿Qué hizo el Hermano Tacumá? (2)
5. ¿Qué sugerencia le dio el Hermano Pájaro al Hermano Tacumá? (2)
6. ¿Qué decidieron hacer? (2)
7. ¿Que hizo el Hermano Pájaro en la noche? (2)
8. ¿Qué descubrieron el Hermano Pájaro y el Hermano Tacumá? (2)

Read the passage carefully and then answer the questions in Spanish **using your own words.**

A Marcos le encantaban los zapatos. siempre quería que sus padres le compraran zapatos nuevos. El tenía varios tipos de zapatos - los zapatos para la iglesia y otras ocasiones formales, los zapatos que llevaba para la escuela, y los que llevaba en casa.

A veces cuando los zapatos todavía estaban nuevos él les decía a sus padres que necesitaba zapatos nuevos. Cada vez que le compraban un par nuevo él escondía un par viejo aunque le sirviera todavía.

Un día su mamá descubrió una caja grande en la cual Marcos había escondido todos los zapatos que no quería llevar. Había seis pares de zapatos en buenas condiciones. Se sorprendió mucho de que su hijo vanidoso hubiera escondido los zapatos para obtener zapatos nuevos. Decidió que iba a "hacerle un truco"

Llevó todos los zapatos al zapatero y le dijo que quería que limpiara los zapatos para que parecieran nuevos. Después llevó los zapatos a la casa y le dijo a Marcos que le había comprado unos zapatos nuevos. Marcos inmediatamente se alegró, cambió los zapatos que llevaba y se puso un par de "los nuevos".

Después de un día todos los zapatos que tenía antes desaparecieron. La mamá sonrió y se dijo:
- Un día esos zapatos van a ser nuevos otra vez.

Preguntas

1. ¿Qué le gustaba a Marcos? (1)
2. ¿Por qué tenía diferentes pares de zapatos? (2)
3. ¿Qué hacía cuando recibió un par de zapatos nuevos? (2)
4. ¿Cómo eran los zapatos que Marcos escondió? (2)
5. ¿Qué hizo la mamá con los zapatos que halló? (2)
6. Cuando Marcos recibió los zapatos 'nuevos', ¿qué hizo? (2)
7. ¿Qué pasó con los zapatos que tenía antes? (2)
8. ¿Qué dijo la mamá a sí misma? (2)

Read the passage carefully and then answer the questions in Spanish **using your own words.**

Llegaron bastante temprano a la playa, como a los ocho de la mañana. Todavía no había nadie allí y el cielo estaba nublado.
- Vamos a nadar ahora - dijo Ricardo a sus compañeros.
- No quiero - respondió Marianela. El agua va a estar fría. Prefiero esperar hasta las diez.
- Bueno, yo te acompaño - dijo Kamal.

Al ver a sus dos amigos entrar en el agua, Marianela cambió de idea y como ya tenía puesto el traje de baño, saltó al agua.

Bajo la superficie del mar veían un mundo maravilloso con peces de colores, unos con colas largas, otros pequeños. De repente apareció un tiburón. Los niños no sabían qué hacer. No podían apartar sus ojos de los dientes agudos. Se dieron cuenta de que habían nadado muy lejos de la playa.

Parecía que el tiburón quería algo y que no era agresivo. Kamal, el más valiente, se acercó al tiburón y lo tocó. Al animal le gustaba la atención y empezó a moverse suavemente. Luego, nadando lentamente, dejó a los niños. Afortunadamente una canoa con pescadores pasaba cerca de los chicos y los hombres ofrecieron llevarlos a la playa. Los chicos dieron las gracias a los pescadores y decidieron que nunca iban a mencionar a nadie su aventura con el tiburón simpático.

Preguntas

1. ¿Qué tiempo hacía cuando los chicos llegaron a la playa? (1)
2. ¿Por qué no quería Marianela entrar en el agua? (2)
3. ¿Dónde estaban los niños cuando apareció el tiburón? (2)
4. ¿Cómo sabemos que Kamal es valiente? (2)
5. ¿Quiénes ayudaron a los niños? (2)
6. ¿Cómo regresaron a la playa los chicos? (2)
7. ¿Qué pensaban los niños del tiburón? (2)
8. ¿Qué decidieron los niños? (2)

Read the passage carefully and then answer the questions in Spanish **using your own words.**

Yolanda llegó a casa, subió corriendo las escaleras y llamó a la puerta del dormitorio de su hermano. Entró sin esperar respuesta. Su hermano estaba tendido en la cama leyendo y escuchando música.

- Por favor, Esteban, quiero que me escuches. Tengo algo muy importante que decirte.
Esteban no quería apagar la grabadora pero se dio cuenta de que su hermana menor estaba muy nerviosa y decidió hacerle caso.

- ¿Qué te pasa, Yolanda?
- Pues, esta tarde, camino de la casa, vi algo muy raro en el parque. Había un hombre, vestido de negro, agachado cerca de unas matas. Parecía que trataba de esconder algo, quizás un paquete. Me metí detrás de un árbol y lo miré por unos minutos. Por fin se levantó y salió sin el paquete. Esteban, yo tengo que saber qué hay en el paquete. Los hermanos decidieron salir de la casa durante la noche, cuando sus padres dormían.

Al llegar la hora, los dos salieron de la casa de puntillas y corrieron hacia el parque. Empezaron a buscar el paquete en la oscuridad y acababan de hallarlo cuando, de repente, oyeron unos pasos acercándose rápidamente.

Los jóvenes se asustaron y no sabían qué hacer. Se miraron temblando sin poder hablar. ¡Eran sus padres! Los hermanos tuvieron que regresar a casa inmediatamente, dejando atrás el paquete. Nunca supieron qué había adentro pero todavía creen que era bastante dinero para hacerles ricos durante toda la vida.

Preguntas

1. ¿Qué hizo Yolanda al subir las escaleras? (1)
2. ¿Por qué decidió el hermano escuchar a Yolanda? (2)
3. ¿Por qué estaba preocupada Yolanda? (2)
4. ¿Qué hacía el hombre que Yolanda observaba? (2)
5. ¿Qué decisión tomaron los hermanos? (2)
6. ¿Qué ocurrió cuando hallaron el paquete? (2)
7. ¿Cómo se sentían los dos jóvenes? (2)
8. ¿Qué pasó cuando sus padres llegaron? (2)

Read the passage carefully and then answer the questions in Spanish **using your own words**.

> Mi queridísima tía,
>
> No quiero que mi mamá sepa lo que te voy a decir porque va a enojarse pero ando en apuros.
>
> Hace quince días, iba en mi motocicleta cuando de repente apareció un hombre frente a mí. No pude evitarlo. Él dijo que estaba en el paso de peatones cuando ocurrió el accidente pero no lo creo. Lo llevaron a la clínica y tengo que pagar las cuentas porque dicen que tengo la culpa.
>
> La policía llegó al lugar del accidente y me arrestaron acusándome de ser responsable porque según ellos yo había excedido la velocidad permitida. Estoy seguro que eso tampoco es verdad.
>
> Tuve que pasar la noche en la cárcel y me llevaron la mañana siguiente al tribunal. Para colmo de desgracias la juez me acusó de conducir de una manera peligrosa y a una velocidad excesiva y me multó con dos mil quinientos dólares.
>
> Por favor tía, ayúdame. También tengo que reparar mi motocicleta, comprar comida y con las otras cuentas necesito diez mil dólares. Te los voy a devolver en cuanto encuentre trabajo. ¡Ojalá sea pronto!
>
> Gracias querida tía y espero una carta con el dinero lo antes posible.
>
> Recibe un abrazo cariñoso de tu sobrino,
>
> Ronaldo.

Preguntas

1. ¿Por qué la mamá de Ronaldo no debe saber lo que ha ocurrido? (1)
2. ¿Dónde estaba el hombre cuando ocurrió el accidente? (2)
3. ¿Por qué tiene que pagar Ronaldo las cuentas de la clínica? (2)
4. ¿Cuánto tiempo pasó Ronaldo encarcelado? (2)
5. Para Ronaldo, ¿qué fue lo peor que le ocurrió? (2)
6. ¿Cuánto tuvo que pagar Ronaldo en el tribunal? (2)
7. ¿Por qué Ronaldo no tiene dinero para pagar sus cuentas? (2)
8. ¿Cuándo quiere Ronaldo recibir el dinero de su tía? (2)

Read the passage carefully and then answer the questions in Spanish **using your own words**.

El hermano Tigre estaba muy orgulloso de su finca. Las plantas crecían muy rápidamente y él esperaba el día cuando pudiera comer algo que él mismo había cultivado.

Por fin llegó el día cuando decidió que todo estaba listo para recoger la cosecha. Iba a cortar el plátano cuando el plátano le habló tranquilamente diciéndole:

- Haga el favor de no cortarme.

El Hermano Tigre estaba tan asustado que tiró el machete al suelo. Pero, poco después agarró el machete de nuevo para destruir la planta. Al levantar la mano, el machete le habló también y le dijo:
- Por favor no me uses para cortarla.

Eso fue demasiado para el Hermano Tigre quien echó a correr. Corrió a toda velocidad hasta la casa del Hermano Anansi para contarle su fantástica historia. El Hermano Anansi le dio agua fría para calmarle. Después de dos o tres minutos, El Hermano Tigre le contó lo que le había pasado. El Hermano Anansi empezó a reírse. Entonces El Hermano Anansi le dijo al Hermano Tigre que era un cobarde y que era muy estúpido tener miedo de una planta.

Entonces el Hermano Anansi decidió preparar una comida para los dos. Mientras arreglaba la leña para encender el fuego se burlaba del Hermano Tigre. En medio de las risas, la leña le preguntó:
- ¿Por qué te burlas del pobre Hermano Tigre?
Dicen que el Hermano Anansi todavía está corriendo.

Preguntas

1. ¿Qué esperaba hacer el Hermano Tigre? (1)
2. ¿Qué ocurrió cuando iba a cosechar el plátano? (2)
3. ¿Cómo reaccionó el Hermano Tigre? (2)
4. ¿Qué decidió hacer después? (2)
5. Cuando iba a hacerlo, ¿qué hizo el machete? (2)
6. ¿A quién fue a contar la historia? (2)
7. ¿Qué le dijo esa persona? (2)
8. ¿Qué se dice del Hermano Anansi? (2)

Read the passage carefully and then answer the questions in Spanish **using your own words.**

Los garífunas

Los garífunas constituyen un grupo étnico disperso a lo largo de las costas de cinco países de Centroamérica. No están seguros de todos los detalles precisos de su génesis pero están de acuerdo en que su historia comienza a principios del siglo xvii, cuando dos barcos que transportaban esclavos de África Occidental al Nuevo Mundo naufragaron cerca de San Vicente, en las islas de Barlovento. Los africanos que sobrevivieron fueron acogidos por los indios caribes que habitaban la isla. Con el tiempo ambos grupos se mezclaron y originaron a los garífunas.

Los garífunas a quienes los ingleses llamaban "caribes negros" para distinguirlos de los nativos de América Central, constituyeron un orgulloso pueblo que resistió la colonización por más de cien años. Después de una serie de guerras y levantamientos contra los ingleses, sus principales dirigentes fueron capturados. Los victoriosos ingleses decidieron deportarlos a la inhóspita isla de Roatán, frente a Honduras. Desde allí, los refugiados garífunas se extendieron a distintos lugares de Centroamérica, estableciéndose principalmente en Honduras, Guatemala y Belice, que se denominaba Honduras Británica hasta su independencia en 1981.

En la actualidad alrededor de doscientos mil garífunas viven en Honduras, unos quince mil en Belice, seis mil en Guatemala y otros pocos miles en las islas de Barlovento y Nicaragua. Aunque están separados por fronteras nacionales, los garífunas se mantienen unidos en su determinación por preservar su cultura, rica en influencias africanas y americanas.

Las comunidades garífunas conservan celosamente su arte, su música, sus artesanías y sus creencias religiosas, que en conjunto constituyen una forma de vida muy particular.

Preguntas

1. ¿Dónde se encuentran a los garífunas? (1)
2. ¿Cuándo empieza la historia de los garífunas? (2)
3. ¿Cómo llegaron a San Vicente? (2)
4. ¿Cómo se originaron los garífunas? (2)
5. ¿Por qué los ingleses los llamaban "caribes negros"? (2)
6. ¿Cómo llegaron los garífunas a Roatán? (2)

7. ¿Cuántos garífunas viven en Guatemala y en Belice respectivamente? (2)
8. ¿En qué país se encuentra la población más grande de garífunas? (2)

DIRECTED WRITING

GENERAL PROFICIENCY

Candidates are required to write a passage of 80 - 100 words based on written cues.

This section corresponds to **Paper 2, Section 4 and is worth 20 marks.**

GENERAL PROFICIENCY

Paper 2 - Section 4

Use the information provided in each set of cues to write in Spanish a paragraph of **80 -100 words**. Be sure to include all the information given.

1. la familia Mendoza / deseo de salir / el teatro Mundo Nuevo / la taquilla / un drama interesante / seis actores / una nueva actriz famosa / aplausos / situaciones cómicas / una fiesta después.

2. a la medianoche / voces y gritos / un fuego / sonido de las sirenas / los bomberos / problemas con la manguera / la ventana / ayuda / toda la aldea / nadie herido.

3. 11:30 de la noche / una pensión antigua / ningún monedero / mucha hambre / ninguna tarjeta de crédito / un propietario simpático / alojamiento y comida / un cuarto cómodo / buena suerte / agradecidos.

4. en el aeropuerto / un piloto borracho / las azafatas en huelga / pasajeros furiosos / colas largas / vuelos atrasados / una disputa / dos pasajeros / una azafata / disculpas.

5. un grupo de turistas / una expedición / una guía / mucha experiencia / varios países / muchos tesoros / el mar calmado / un mapa de la zona / gran éxito / una gran celebración.

6. un almacén / el administrador / un trabajo difícil / tiempo libre / muchos departamentos / muchos clientes / poco dinero / productos caros / empleados perezosos / desastre.

7. 2 de la tarde / un día hermoso de abril / niños y mayores / debajo de los árboles / un niñito perdido / la comisaría / una llamada telefónica / los padres del niño / agradecimiento / recompensa.

8. dos novios / un día espléndido / la puesta del sol / un café francés / el cine / una película divertida / una heladería / un mendigo / el resto del dinero / felices.

9. las 4 de la tarde / una familia numerosa / alrededor de la mesa / la campana de la iglesia / hacia la iglesia / una escena horrible / la figura

de un hombre / la ventana / una escalera / aplausos.

10. un muchacho tímido / chileno / de visita en México / una familia mexicana / un vecino antipático / un gato muerto / en el jardín / todos asustados / ayuda / agradecimiento.

11. dos amigos juntos / camino de casa / en la esquina / un toro / mala suerte / un toro ferroz / un árbol cercano / sorpresa / un toro tímido / poco miedo.

12. el verano pasado / María / sus compañeros de clase / un viaje / España / los autobuses / un accidente / un carro alquilado / muchos edificios de esplendor / un tiempo fantástico.

13. en el banco / un viejo / una cuenta de ahorros / ningún dinero / una cajera simpática / un error / mucho dinero / una lotería especial / muchos regalos / obras de caridad.

14. camino del parque / un pinchazo / una llamada al mecánico / un mecánico descuidoso / cinco minutos después / otro pinchazo / ayuda de un taxista / un trabajo excelente / otro pinchazo / ¡mal día!.

15. ayer/durante el recreo / un regalo para la profesora / una caja grande / otra caja grande / una rana grande / profesora asustada / niños traviesos / la oficina del director / dos días sin el recreo.

16. fiesta de cumpleaños / muchos regalos / una torta grande / dos niños y una niña / diez velas / un soplo fuerte / el mantel encendido / mucha agua / torta dañada / celebraciones todavía.

17. 3:15 de la tarde / en coche / luces de tráfico / la luz en rojo / unos niños / de regreso de la escuela / conversación animada / caída en la calle / un accidente / ambulancia.

18. casa tranquila / ruidos / la cocina / un ladrón vestido de negro / una lucha / dos ladrones más / muebles rotos / una persona muerta / sirenas y la policía / la comisaría.

19. el fin de semana / buen tiempo / la playa / mucha gente / almuerzo delicioso / el mar y las olas / un hombre en peligro / ayuda / respiración artificial / recuperación.

20. en bote/ unos amigos / una tarde agradable / el motor descompuesto / la noche / una luz a lo lejos / pescadores / canoas / ayuda/ regreso a la playa.

21. 8:00 de la mañana / la familia ocupada / en coche / camino del aeropuerto / los boletos en casa / el regreso / la búsqueda frenética / llegada tarde / salida del avión / desilusión.

22. dos equipos / entrenamiento durante las tardes / el gran día / el partido emocionante / la muchedumbre / un gol disputado / golpes / lucha / jugadores y espectadores / la decisión del árbitro.

23. la escuela secundaria / en la clase de español / un chico travieso / una broma con un ratón / mucha risa / la profesora enojada / la oficina del director / carta / los padres / el castigo.

24. en un bote pequeño / muchas personas / lejos de la playa / ruidos en el motor / de noche / oscuridad / miedo / por fin una luz / pescadores simpáticos / regreso a la playa.

25. de compras / el nuevo centro comercial / muchas tiendas / ropa y zapatos / la cafetería / al aire libre / helado y pastel / las seis de la tarde / el coche robado / regreso a la casa.

26. la disco / música y baile / ropa de moda / un cantante fantástico / las luces apagadas / gritos / confusión / la salida cerrada / muchos heridos / una noche inolvidable.

27. mamá / de compras / los hijitos con el papá en casa / los hijitos en el jardín / juegos / papá con el cigarrillo / un fósforo en la alfombra / un incendio / los bomberos / mamá enojada.

28. ayer / en el supermercado / muchas cosas en los estantes / la carretilla llena / la cuenta enorme / el dinero perdido / la cajera enojada / la llegada del gerente / lágrimas / a casa sin nada.

29. la fiesta de cumpleaños / mucha comida y bebida / dolor de estómago / el consultorio del médico / la recepcionista / preguntas del médico / examinación / la receta / aspirinas y antibióticos / en cama por unos días

30. el huracán / relámpago y trueno / lluvia / muebles mojados / techo destruido / agua por todas partes / miedo / todos confundidos / la situación afuera / los vecinos.

31. anteayer / en coche / el campo / el camino desierto / mucha lluvia / limpiaparabrisas rotos / la llanta pinchada / una casa a lo lejos / la familia simpática / ayuda.

32. a las orillas del río / peces grandes / pensamientos de la comida / el pez enorme / en medio del río / el agua profunda / caída al agua / un ramo / la espera larga / salvado por un extranjero.

33. durante las vacaciones / juegos / un niño en la piscina / el agua tibia y agradable / mucha diversión / ¡Socorro! / un hombre en un banco / una llamada telefónica / una ambulancia / el hospital Cifuentes.

34. la semana pasada / un supermercado moderno / una mujer gorda / una disputa en voz alta / una dieta estricta / la sección de verduras / mucha comida deliciosa / el horario de comer / la ayuda de una buena amiga / una gran celebración.

35. el restaurante Altamira / camareros simpáticos / mesas vacías / 2 borrachos / una lucha / muebles rotos / heridos / el gerente / un camarero / la policía.

36. buen tiempo / invitaciones a todos los vecinos / una fiesta / una comida deliciosa / música y baile / llegada de un extranjero / gritos / sorpresa / un primo de Michigan / celebraciones.

37. fin de semana / una fiesta / 27 estudiantes y dos profesores / comida chilena / muchas decoraciones / las chicas en ropa elegante / música jamaiquina / demasiado ruido / los vecinos / el director de la escuela.

38. un día espléndido / la familia Mendoza / el parque / flores y un lago / muchas otras personas / juegos divertidos / una llave perdida / el coche cerrado / un autobús / al parque otra vez.

39. 11:30 de la noche / ruidos abajo / las escaleras / un desconocido / el armario / un cuchillo grande / el escape / la ventana del dormitorio / en un árbol / toda la noche.

40. 3 de marzo / por la tarde / la dueña de la joyería / atraco por hombres enmascarados / todo el dinero y muchas joyas / un hombre famoso herido / la sala de emergencia / médicos y enfermeros / un detective / reportaje en el periódico.

41. en la tienda / una postal de felicitación / el empleado amable / jóvenes enamorados / letra original / colores brillantes / pinturas lindas / mucho dinero / una perfecta / en el Correos.

42. un niño antipático / una niña simpática / todos los días / camino de la escuela / insectos muertos / un día después de las clases / la niña frustrada / venganza / disculpas / buenos amigos al fin.

43. las 9 de la noche / en una casa hermosa / un niño de seis años / el sillón de la abuela / los fantasmas / las sombras / sonidos extraños / fantasía / la risa / sueño.

44. el paso de peatones / un coche / a toda velocidad / un grupo de estudiantes / el ganado / un choque / una vaca muerta / cuatro niños heridos / el granjero triste / la gente enojada.

45. el domingo en la noche / el teatro / un concierto fantástico / un gran pianista / el piano dañado / el pianista mal vestido / todo el mundo ansioso / una espera larga / el pianista confundido / una catástrofe.

46. 31 de diciembre / en el teatro / la Nochevieja / una cola delante de la taquilla / a mitad de la obra de teatro / un programa interesante / una actriz en el suelo / el público emocionado / aplausos / mucha diversión.

47. durante las vacaciones / un circo / tres monos / dos payasos / saltos / un elefante enojado / el dueño asustado / un bebé en un cochecito / dos guardias / una cesta de frutas / gritos.

48. los veraneantes / la hora de comer / una cafetería / frutas, gaseosas y cerveza / debajo de un toldo / mucha gente / las tres y cuarto / el autobús / la salida.

49. el cielo claro / mucho caos / enfrente de un restaurante / dos señores / un camarero / llamada por teléfono / la comida en la mesa / otros clientes curiosos / los gritos del chófer / las risas.

50. el estadio / muchos aficionados / la corrida de toros / un aficionado borracho / el toro cansado / los oficiales asustados / el toro furioso / el aficionado en el suelo / el toro con la ropa del hombre / risas y gritos.

51. medianoche / un autobús viejo / en la oscuridad / un accidente / el chofer herido / los pasajeros furiosos / el cura / un aldeano simpático / ayuda de todos en la aldea / hasta las 4 de la madrugada.

52. una fiesta de cumpleaños / una banda de músicos / bailarines / un invitado borracho / una lucha / mucho ruido / los vecinos / la policía / celebración interrumpida / gran desilusión.

53. el hospital / un hombre extraño / una enfermera / dos médicos / el gerente del hospital / papeles de identificación / el guardia / un paciente tímido / mucho dolor / mucha medicina.

54. 12:30 de la tarde / en la pescadería / un mendigo / una cesta grande / los mejores peces / el dueño simpático / una muchedumbre de clientes / el mendigo tímido / pescado gratis / gratitud.

55. ayer / un cliente / en la sastrería / un traje formal / las medidas / muchas demandas / muchos bolsillos / demasiado dinero / el sastre enojado / el traje por la ventana.

www.ingramcontent.com/pod-product-compliance
Lightning Source LLC
LaVergne TN
LVHW061342060426
835512LV00016B/2631